WALKING
—THROUGH—
DARTMOOR'S
PAST

MICHAEL BENNIE

With maps and illustrations by Jonathan Bennie

Peninsula
Press

Published by Peninsula Press Ltd
P.O. Box 31
Newton Abbot
Devon TQ12 5XH

Tel: 01803 875875

Printed in England by
The Cromwell Press, Trowbridge, Wiltshire.

ISBN 1 872640 45 1

CONTENTS

Introduction

The history of man's association with Dartmoor is a story of gradual change and development, of evolution rather than revolution. Nothing that has happened here has dramatically changed the course of history: no major battles, no political plots, no earth-shaking events. Indeed, few of the major players in Britain's history seem to have paid it much attention at all.

That is not to say, of course, that Dartmoor does not have a history - it does, and a fascinating history at that. But it was shaped by ordinary people - farmers, workers, small businessmen - rather than by kings and queens, politicians and statesmen. And in a way that makes exploring its past all the more interesting; one can more easily identify with the people and their activities, and it is easier to trace the changes that have occurred over the centuries.

This book contains a variety of walks, long and short, easy and more challenging, which visit some of the sites associated with Dartmoor's past, tracing the major developments from about 2000 BC to the twentieth century, from farming and mining to administration and religion. The criteria I have used in choosing each walk are the interest of the site (what there is to see and how representative it is of the period or activity it illustrates), the feasibility of the route and the beauty and variety of the scenery through which it passes.

At the beginning of each walk, I give a brief explanation of the background or history of the site to be visited. Since this is a walking guide not a history book, I have not gone into too much detail; the aim has been simply to give you a flavour of the period or activity described. If you would like to find out more about Dartmoor's past, there is a Bibliography at the back of the book which lists the publications I have found most interesting and useful, and to which you might like to refer.

All the walks are circular, and at the start of each route description there is information on where each walk starts, its length and the approximate time it takes. And I must stress that these times *are* only approximate. They are an indication of the time a reasonably fit person might take to complete the walk and take no account of time spent exploring the site or of lunch and other breaks. Some of the routes overlap, and where this is the case I indicate which other ones they link with in case you want to combine two walks to make a longer expedition.

I also indicate where you can park if you are driving, but bearing in mind the problems that large numbers of cars can cause to a fragile environment like Dartmoor, you may like to take advantage of the excellent bus services which link the surrounding towns and villages with the moor. The winter schedule is somewhat limited, but in summer there are frequent services to most of the more popular access points.

I have graded the routes according to difficulty: A means short and easy, relatively flat and along well-defined paths or roads; B means rather longer, perhaps over open ground and with one or two moderately steep ascents; and C means rather more challenging - usually over 12km (7$^1/_2$ miles), probably with some fairly steep climbs and a certain amount of rough terrain. Sketch maps are provided, but the best Ordnance Survey map to use is the Outdoor Leisure one, No 28 (Dartmoor), with a scale of 1:25,000.

Finally, three words of warning. First, the weather on Dartmoor is fickle - it can change with remarkable speed and with very little warning. So if you are going any distance at all, you should be prepared for all conditions, and you should let someone know your route in case they need to call out the rescue service.

Secondly, it is not a good idea for those without the requisite navigation skills to venture out onto the open moor in the mist. There are few landmarks, and in poor visibility one tor looks much like another. It is therefore easy to become lost and disoriented.

And thirdly, although only one of the walks in this book (Walk 5) takes you onto a military range, you should be aware that a large area of the northern moor is used for military training, and that live firing takes place from time to time. If you are thinking of extending your walk into those areas, therefore, you should find out the times of firing. Details of where to find the necessary information are given in the route summary for Walk 5. On no account venture onto the ranges (marked by red and white poles and notice boards) when there are red flags flying from the nearby hills.

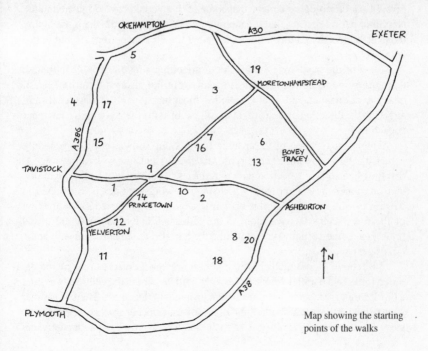

Map showing the starting points of the walks

1. Ancient Rituals

MERRIVALE STONE ROWS

THE BACKGROUND

Over 70 stone rows have been identified on Dartmoor, as well as numerous stone circles (known as sanctuaries) and standing stones (menhirs), yet their origins and functions remain something of a mystery. It is difficult to date them with any certainty; archaeologists believe that some of them could have originated in the Neolithic period, but it is now generally agreed that most of them, including those at Merrivale, date from what is called the Beaker period, around 2500-2000 BC.

Most of the stone rows on Dartmoor are either single or double, although there are some triple ones. There is usually (but not always) a cairn or burial chamber at one end, and what is called a 'blocking stone' - a stone set at right angles to the direction of the row - at the other. In some there is a burial chamber at each end.

The exact function of these stone rows is not known, but it is generally agreed that they had some ritual purpose, and their association with cairns suggests that they had some connection with burial rites. At one time it was thought that their alignment was significant - perhaps following ley lines or connected in some way with the sun - but this view is now generally rejected. The direction of the rows seems to have more to do with geography than with any ritual importance - they usually run uphill, and the burial sites are almost always at the top of the row.

Just above Merrivale there is the largest and most diverse ritual site on the moor. It has two parallel double stone rows, with a cairn in the centre of one, and a third, single, row running south-west at an angle to the others. There is another single row a little to the south of the main site, but since it consists of only three stones it is not easy to identify. Also to the south of the rows are a sanctuary and

6

a menhir, both of which must also have had some ritual or religious purpose, although as with the stone rows it is not known just what that purpose was.

The area must have been a fairly important burial site, since there are several cairns and a kistvaen (a burial chamber without a cairn or barrow covering it) associated with the stone rows themselves, and a further 13 are known to have existed in the surrounding area.

THE WALK

Start and finish: The car park at the top of the hill just east of Merrivale Bridge. Grid reference 553750
Parking: In the car park
Length: 8km (5 miles)
Approximate time: 2$^1/_2$ hours
Degree of difficulty: B
Links with: Walk 14
Route summary: This walk takes you up onto the open moor to visit the most extensive ritual remains on Dartmoor. You then carry on up to a couple of old granite quarries, with some magnificent views as you go, and return along pretty country lanes and farm tracks. There are a few climbs and one or two areas can become wet and muddy after rain, but the route is generally fairly easy.

Take the well-worn path away from the road, in the general direction of the television mast you can see rising above the horizon. As the path peters out, aim slightly to the right of the mast to reach the stone rows. As you go, you will notice the remains of a number of Bronze Age huts to your left (for more on Bronze Age settlements, see Walk 2). As you reach the brow of the hill, you will see the first of the stone rows laid out in front of you, with the blocking stone standing out to your left. There is a leat on the other side, and beyond that is the second stone row, also with its blocking stone clearly visible at the left-hand end.

Turn and follow the second row to the right and you will see a kistvaen (a burial chamber) on the left. The central covering rock is missing, enabling one to see into the chamber. It is fairly small, but large enough to hold someone in a crouching position. Just beyond the kistvaen you will see a burial mound in the centre of the stone row itself. Turn left, south from the stone row, to reach the sanctuary and the standing stone which are clearly visible in front of the wall ahead of you.

Follow the line of the wall to the left. Where it turns to the right, follow it, crossing a stream as you do so. You may have to go a little way upstream to find a suitable crossing point, and you should take care after rain as it can become rather wet underfoot. After crossing the stream, follow the wall up the hill towards the tor up ahead, which is King's Tor.

Before you reach the tor itself, you will come to a track which follows the line of a loop in the Plymouth and Dartmoor Railway. This line started at Princetown and transported granite from the quarries in the area down to Plymouth for shipment to London and elsewhere (see Walk 14). There is a very good view to the right over the northern moor. Follow the track through a cutting as it curves to the left round King's Tor. As you do so, another superb view opens up ahead of you.

Soon you will see the spoil tips of Swelltor Quarries, which used to be one of the major granite quarries on this side of Dartmoor, half left. Where the track forks, take the left-hand fork to reach the quarry itself. Commercial quarrying started in this area in about 1780, although Swelltor's main working life was in the late nineteenth and early twentieth centuries. As you follow this track, you will come across several corbels alongside it. These were quarried and carved

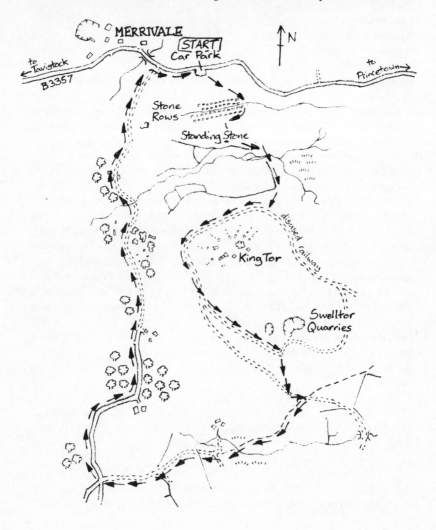

here for use in the widening of London Bridge in 1903, but were found to be surplus to requirements and simply left by the side of the railway. (For more on quarrying, see Walk 13.) In the quarry itself you will see the remains of some of the old quarry buildings.

Follow the track through the quarry, and where it ends, turn right to go down to the fence on the other side of the lower track. Turn left, and after a short distance you will find a gate with a public bridlepath sign on the right. Go through the gate and follow the path down the hill through the gorse and through a gap in a wall. Be careful along here, as it becomes rather muddy after rain.

The path is fairly clear, but to help you find your way there are blue waymarks painted on some of the rocks. After a while, you will also see posts marked with blue arrows. You should find yourself heading for a large tor (Ingra Tor) on the horizon. Cross a stream, still following the waymarked rocks and posts.

Soon after crossing the stream, the path joins a track. Bear left (in fact almost straight on) and follow the track to a gate. Go through it and continue for about 400m until the track joins a lane. Follow the lane across a cattle grid and down a hill. At the crossroads, turn right (signposted to Daveytown).

This lane winds gently down between hedges to cross a river, and then climbs gently up the other side of the valley. It ends at Daveytown farm. Go straight on up the track ahead (signposted to Merrivale), through three gates in quick succession, and then after a little while through a fourth. The track continues to climb through some trees, with an old wall on your left for most of the way.

At the end of the climb, go through a gate. The track now levels off and winds among some rocks before crossing a river. Shortly after the crossing, go through two gates, with a rather muddy patch in between, into a farmyard. Cross the farmyard to a roughly surfaced track on the other side. As you walk along this stretch, you can see the River Walkham cascading down on your left, and the old Dartmoor Inn at Merrivale half-left. Go through a gate into another farmyard, and across to a road. Turn right and follow the road up the hill back to the car park.

2. Bronze Age Herdsmen

BRONZE AGE REAVE, NEAR VENFORD RESERVOIR

THE BACKGROUND

In terms of population at least, the Bronze Age (the period from about 2000 to 500 BC) could almost be regarded as a golden age for Dartmoor. Apart from the highest ground, the area was probably considerably more wooded than it is now, and the climate was somewhat milder. There was therefore quite a good living to be had from the moor: there was grazing for livestock, deer to be hunted, wood and peat for fuel, stone for housing, and plenty of water. There was also some cultivation in the lower-lying areas.

Some idea of the extent of Bronze Age settlement of the area can be gained from the fact that the remains of about 4,000 huts from this period have been identified, with the main influx of settlers arriving around 1700 BC.

These huts were almost always circular, with low walls about 1.2m (4ft) high and up to 2.5m (8ft) thick. The walls were built of stone on the inside, with the cracks filled with dry stone masonry, backed by earth, and with large stones or banks of earth on the outside. There were also some wooden huts, although of course there is now no trace of these above ground. The topsoil inside the huts was removed, so that the floor was below the level of the ground outside. The roofs were conical and consisted of turf, heather or rushes supported by a central post and rafters. Sleeping platforms have been found in some huts, but it appears that in most of them the occupants slept on the floor. The entrances were low and narrow - not usually more than about 1m (3ft) high or wide - and paved, and some were screened by an extension to the main wall. They always faced away from the coldest winds - i.e. in any direction except north or north-west. Some huts were enclosed within their own courtyards, while others were open to the moor. A few huts, including one on this walk, even had interior divisions, perhaps indicating a developing desire for privacy.

Cooking was done on granite slabs set into the floors of the huts, sometimes in the middle and sometimes against a wall. There were usually cooking holes alongside them; these were simply holes in the ground which served as crude ovens and were kept hot by stones which were heated on the fire.

There is a variety of settlement patterns: some of the huts stand alone and isolated; some are grouped in small but scattered settlements; and others, like those at Rider's Rings above the Avon Dam and Grimspound on the slopes of Hamel Down, have outer walls, some of which would have been extremely thick and high, enclosing a large number of huts. The huts we can see on this walk generally fall into the second category; they do not form close-knit communities as at Grimspound, but they are close enough together to form a settlement of sorts.

Some time around 1600 or 1700 BC boundary works known as reaves were constructed, comprising banks, ditches and even some timber fences. It appears that there were two kinds: territorial reaves, which probably marked the boundaries of large tracts of pasture land, usually based on river valleys and watersheds; and much smaller enclosures, which probably served as fields. Examples of both kinds are visible on this walk. It has been suggested that the territorial reaves might have been constructed by some kind of elite 'aristocracy' to delineate the borders of their respective areas, but there is no direct evidence of this. It has also been suggested that our Bronze Age ancestors might have practised transhumance - bringing their livestock to Dartmoor from other areas to graze in the summer. Whatever their origin, the existence of the reaves does seem to suggest that the pressure of an increasing population necessitated the delineation of territorial boundaries of some kind.

A major climatic change is believed to have made Dartmoor colder and bleaker between about 1000 and 500 BC, and people gradually abandoned the high ground. Only a few settlements on the fringes of the moor remained into the Iron Age.

THE WALK

Start and finish: Combestone Tor. Grid reference: 670717
Parking: There is a car park at Combestone Tor.
Length: 5km (3 miles)
Approximate time: 1½ hours
Degree of difficulty: B
Links with: Walks 8 and 10
Route summary: This walk gives you a real feel for the open moor without having to go too far to enjoy it. There are some excellent views and a wealth of Bronze Age remains to be seen along the way. But although it is a fairly short route, there are few clear paths, and it is therefore not one to be undertaken in bad visibility unless you have the necessary navigational skills.

Cross the road and follow the broad, grassy path leading off straight ahead, with a bank on the left. This bank is a reave, part of an extensive system on this part of the moor. After just over 100m you will see the remains of a Bronze Age hut on your left, set in its own enclosure and with an internal dividing wall. Keep following the reave, and about 250m beyond the first hut circle, you will come to a second, also with its own enclosure.

About 50m beyond this second hut circle, you will come to a fairly substantial reave running at right angles to the path you are on. This was probably a territorial reave. Turn left and follow it until it crosses a grassy track. If you look to your right here, you will see a burial mound and beyond it a cross. Turn right along the track and make for the cross. This is Horn's Cross, one of a series erected to mark the ancient route across the moor for monks travelling from Buckfast Abbey to Tavistock Abbey (see Walk 8).

Follow the path past the cross. The views are superb from here, virtually through 360 degrees. Soon you will see Venford Reservoir over to your left, with

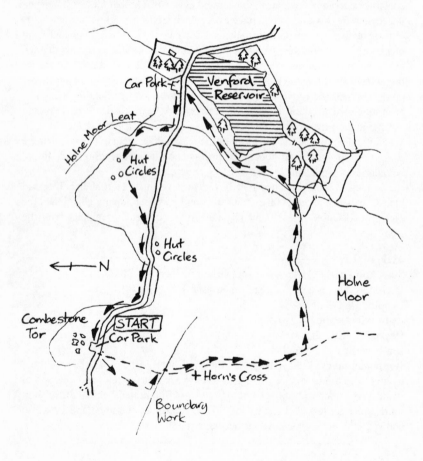

a valley and a stream running down towards it. Turn left and follow the stream down. After rain you may have to pick your way through the wet patches. As you go down, you will pass the remains of old tin workings running up from the stream. (For more on tin mining, see Walk 10.)

Keep to the left of the stream all the way down. Towards the bottom you will come to a fence marking the boundary of South West Water's land at Venford Reservoir. Turn left and follow the fence until it takes a right turn. Go straight on. You will cross several reaves as you go, and there are more up to your left. In fact, this whole area is criss-crossed with reaves, and since it is open access land, you can wander at will among them. There are also a few hut circles, but they are not very well preserved and may be difficult to identify.

You should keep generally parallel to Venford Reservoir as you walk through the reaves. You will cross another tin working, and then a road will appear ahead of you. Aim for the car park at the end of the bridge across the reservoir.

Turn left and about 150m from the car park you will see a leat running half right away from the road. Turn off and follow it until it crosses a reave. Turn left and follow the reave. Where it goes to the right, go half-left. There are more reaves up here, interspersed with more recent field boundaries, and also some more hut circles.

Soon you will see the road on your left, leading up to Combestone Tor. Make your way to it, turn right and follow it back to the car park.

3. Iron Age Farmers

ROUND POUND

THE BACKGROUND

The use of iron in Britain probably resulted from two factors: the spread of the requisite skills to the existing Bronze Age population through trade with the rest of Europe; and an influx of new immigrants. These immigrants came in two waves, called Iron Age A and Iron Age B. The Iron Age A people, who came first, were peaceful farmers who probably mixed relatively easily with the existing population. The Iron Age B immigration comprised mainly warriors who were interested only in conquest. The remains we visit on this walk are an Iron Age A site, one of very few to be found on Dartmoor. (For more information on the Iron Age B immigrants, see Walk 20.)

The Iron Age is generally reckoned as the period from about 500 BC to the coming of the Romans in the first century BC, but on Dartmoor it can be said to extend to the Dark Ages, since Roman influence in the area appears to have been minimal - they skirted round to the south and north, avoiding the moorland itself. The period saw the introduction of bellows, which enabled metal-workers to achieve the high temperatures in their fires that were needed to smelt the iron ore. And the iron they produced facilitated new agricultural methods, including the clearing of more forests and the cultivation of heavier soils. However, because of the climatic changes which caused the depopulation of large parts of Dartmoor before the coming of the Iron Age, it was mainly in the east of the area, with its drier climate and richer soil, that there were existing farms able to develop the new ideas.

The layout of the settlement around Kestor is similar to that of many of the Bronze Age remains found elsewhere, which is hardly surprising, as it was occupied during that period; there appears to have been an almost seamless transition from the Bronze to the Iron Age in this area. Scattered around Kestor

14

itself are a number of hut circles and field boundaries, but the largest and best preserved remains are at Round Pound, just across the road from the tor. This hut was large - 11.25m (37ft) in diameter - and lay within its own enclosure. The enclosure entrance was to the north-west, and opened onto a track which ran between fields to the stream. Like many of its Bronze Age counterparts, the hut doorway faced south-east and was cobbled. There was a step up on the outside to stop water running into the hut, and three steps down on the inside to the floor. The walls were made of vertical slabs on the inside and horizontal slabs on the outside, with small stones filling the space in between.

The interior of the hut comprised two sections: to the left of the doorway was the living area, with a clean, paved floor and a small hearth. On the opposite side was the working area, with a clay-lined hole for smelting the iron ore, another hole for forging (i.e. reheating after smelting) a third hole over which water was poured onto the iron to quench it, and a granite slab which was used as an anvil. Although these signs of extensive iron-working were all found when the site was first excavated, none of them remains visible today. There may have been a hole in the roof on this side to provide light for working, and also to let the smoke escape.

THE WALK

Start and finish: Gidleigh. Grid reference 670883
Parking: There are several places where you can pull off the road in Gidleigh, including in front of the church. But please be careful that you do not block any gateways.
Length: 8km (5 miles)
Approximate time: $2^1/_2$ hours
Degree of difficulty: B
Route summary: Variety is the keynote of this route, both in the landscapes you walk through and in its historical interest. It takes in woodland, riverbanks, open moor and quiet lanes, with one superb viewpoint. And in addition to the Iron Age complex at Round Pound there are ancient ritual sites to see and you follow in the footsteps of medieval sailors crossing Devon to change ships. It is mostly quite easy walking, although there are one or two fairly stiff climbs.

If you are starting from the church, look through the gate of the house next door before you set off. Just beyond the house are the remains of a fourteenth-century fortified manor house. It is on private property, however, so you cannot go in and explore it.

Follow the road south out of Gidleigh, and at the T-junction turn right (signposted to Berrydown and Scorhill). After about 100m turn left off the road, following the footpath sign for the Mariners' Way to Teigncombe and the road to Kestor Rock. This is the ancient route used by sailors crossing from North to South Devon to join new ships. (For more on ancient routes across Dartmoor, see Walk 8.) Cross a stile and follow the track on the other side.

The track climbs slightly and at the top you go through a gateway and then half right, following the public footpath sign, and almost immediately half left, again following a path sign, off the track onto a path. This leads you down fairly steeply through a conifer plantation towards the North Teign River, which you can hear below you. Keep an eye out as you go and you might just catch a fleeting glimpse of a deer.

You come out onto a track. Turn right, following the footpath sign, and follow the valley of the river. After about 50m, turn left off the track, again following the footpath sign, and cross the river via a footbridge. On the other side, take the path leading straight up the hill for a steep climb through the woods. At the top, go right, and after about 100m or so left, again following the footpath sign, to leave the wood and follow a track.

At the end of the track, you go through a gateway onto a lane. Turn right. There is another climb and at the top you cross a cattle grid out onto the open moor. Keep to the road on the other side, with a good view to the right over the valley. After about 400m you will find the large enclosure of Round Pound on your right, with its hut circle inside. To the left of the enclosure you will see the remains of the field system.

Cross the road and make your way up through the gorse to Kestor. As you go, you will come across more field boundaries and some hut circles. The view from Kestor is quite magnificent, and if you have the energy to climb the rocks, you will get a 360-degree sweep.

If you look over to your right from Kestor, towards the right-hand side of the plantation in the distance, you will see a large stone standing isolated in the middle of the moor. This is the Longstone, part of a complex of prehistoric ritual sites. (For more information on standing stones and stone rows, see Walk 1.) Make your way across to it. In medieval times, it was used as a convenient boundary marker. You can still see the letters DC (for Duke of Cornwall, the owner of Dartmoor Forest) carved on one side and GP (for Gidleigh Parish) on the other. There was once a stone row leading off to the left from it, ending in three standing stones called the Three Boys. There is nothing to be seen of the stone row, and only one of the Three Boys remains, just over the brow of the hill - and that is now almost horizontal.

Turn right from the Longstone to follow the remains of another stone row up the hill. There is not much to be seen of it, just the odd stone. At the top there are the remains of an ancient burial chamber, from which a much clearer stone row runs down the ridge. Towards the end of this stone row and about 15m to the right, you will see another burial chamber, with another stone row running off half right away from it.

Straight ahead of you is yet another stone row. Follow this, aiming for the far end of the wall you can see ahead. There is no actual path beyond the stone row, but it is very easy going, as the grass is short and you can quite clearly see

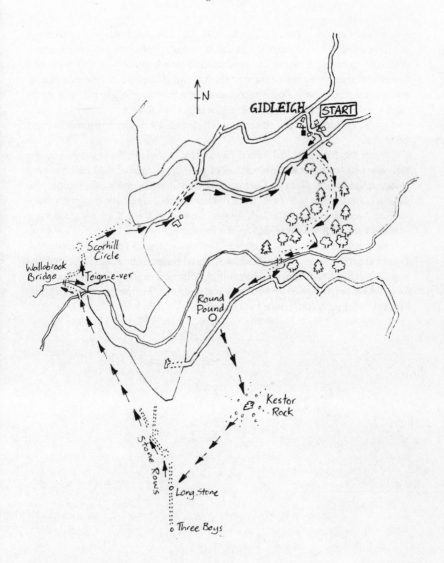

where you are heading. The silence is almost tangible, only occasionally broken by the bleating of a sheep or the call of a meadow pipit.

When you reach the wall, you will see that it goes right down to the North Teign River. Bear left and follow the river upstream for a short distance to a clapper bridge where you can cross. Once across, go left again to another clapper bridge across the Wallabrook. Cross that and make your way back downstream until you are immediately opposite the wall again. Here you will find the Tolmen, a large boulder with a hole right through it. The hole was made by the action of the river when it was higher than it is today; small pebbles were swirled round, gradually grinding away at the boulder over hundreds of years. It was once believed that anyone passing through the hole would be cured of rheumatism. If you are tempted to try it, however, consider how you are going to get back up the bank - and if the river is in spate, it would be foolish to try it at all, as you could end up being washed downstream, which would not do your rheumatism any good at all!

From the Tolmen, head directly away from the river. As you come up the hill, you will see Scorhill Circle ahead of you. This is one of the best-preserved stone circles (see Walk 1) on Dartmoor, containing some substantial stones; the largest is about 2.5m (8ft) high. Turn right at the circle and follow a grassy track leading over the brow of the hill. As you come over the hill, a very good view opens up ahead of you over lush, green farmland.

Go between the two walls ahead of you to a gate, and onto a road beyond. Follow the road down to a junction, and go straight on (signposted to Berrydown and Gidleigh). About 1km (just over mile) further on you will pass the Mariners' Way, which you followed on your way out, leading off to the right. About 100m beyond that, turn left to return to Gidleigh.

– 4. Saxon Administrators and Summary Justice –

LYDFORD CASTLE

THE BACKGROUND

Seeing the sleepy village of Lydford now, it is difficult to imagine that it was once one of the most important towns in Devon. It was a major administrative centre in Saxon times, and was fortified by Alfred the Great as a bulwark against the Cornish and later against the Danes. The Danes actually attacked it in 997, but were beaten off. A few remains of Alfred's defences can still be seen. They consisted of earthworks and timber, with a wooden wall in front; the wall was later replaced by stone.

From 978 to 1050 or perhaps later, it was the site of a royal mint, which produced silver pennies for Knut (Canute), Harold Harefoot, Ethelred the Unready and Edward the Confessor. Specimens of some of these coins can still be seen at the Castle Inn. They show Ethelred on one side and on the other a 'long cross'. This cross was used as a marker when smaller denominations were needed; the coin was literally cut in half or in quarters to provide halfpennies and farthings.

A wooden Norman castle with earth reinforcements was built to the south-west of the church in the latter part of the eleventh century, using part of the original Saxon defences. Lydford's influence declined during this period, however, probably as a result of the building of castles at Okehampton and Launceston, and this castle was soon abandoned. Very little remains to remind us of the village's former importance: the font in the church is believed to be Saxon, and there are a few traces of the original town defences, but apart from the coins, that is all.

The present castle dates back to 1195. It was the official seat of the chief stannary court, where offenders against the tinners' laws (see Walk 9) were tried, and of the forest court, which dealt with offences against the forest laws which applied to Dartmoor. The basement was used as a prison; it was just a 16-foot square pit, with no windows and access only via a ladder. In the sixteenth century, it was described as 'one of the most annoious, contagious and detestable places within this realme'.

Lydford became notorious for 'Lydford Law'; in 1644, the Tavistock poet William Browne wrote:

> I oft have heard of Lydford Law,
> How in the morn they hang and draw
> And sit in judgement after.

This reputation for hanging a man first and trying him afterwards is almost certainly exaggerated. The tale probably originates in the system of courts used to try cases under forest law. Offenders were tried by the Court of Swaincote, which met three times a year, and its verdict was passed up to the Court of Justice Seat for sentence to be passed. However, the Court of Justice Seat only met every three years, and since there was very little doubt that when it did meet, its sentence for certain offences would be death, the forest officials took it upon themselves to hang the offender as soon as the verdict was reached, leaving the court simply to tidy up the paperwork!

Perhaps because of its reputation, Lydford Castle was later associated with Judge Jeffries, who was notorious for his Bloody Assizes. There is no evidence that he ever came to Lydford, but that has not deterred the legend-makers; it is said that he haunts the castle in the form of a black pig.

To the south-west of the village lies Lydford Gorge, a magnificent, steep valley through which flows the River Lyd. It is now a National Trust property, but at one time it was the haunt of an outlaw band known as the Gubbins, who were said to be cannibals.

THE WALK

Start and finish: Lydford, just west of the A386 Tavistock-Okehampton road. Grid reference 510847

Parking: There is a free public car park in the village, opposite the Castle Inn.

Length: The basic route is 4.5km (2¾ miles), but it can be extended to any length you want simply by walking further onto the moor.

Approximate time: 1½ hours

Degree of difficulty: A

Links with: Walk 17

Route summary: After exploring Lydford, this route gives you a small taste of the wildness and spaciousness of Dartmoor with very little effort. The basic route skirts the edge of the moor, but if you are feeling a little more energetic and adventurous you can venture further out and experience the true grandeur of this undeveloped north-western part of the National Park. But if you do venture further onto the moor, remember that this is part of a military range. If there are red flags flying from the nearby tors, it means that there is firing going on and you should not proceed. The basic route does not pass across the range, so that is safe at all times.

From the car park, turn left to visit Lydford Castle. Although it is owned by English Heritage, entry is free and you can explore this gloomy edifice and its dungeon at your leisure. Because it now has no roof, it is difficult, on a bright, sunny day, to imagine the dungeon as it must have been in medieval times.

On leaving the castle, turn right and then immediately right again through a gate. Follow the path round to the left, to reach the remains of the Norman castle. The hedge on your right marks the line of the original Saxon bank. All that remains of this castle are the grassy banks which were once the earth reinforcements to the wooden castle walls.

Return to the road and turn right again to enter the churchyard. The present church was built in the fifteenth century, but it is thought that the first church on the site was founded in the seventh century. There is a delightful inscription on the tomb of George Routleigh, an eighteenth-century watchmaker, just by the church door, which is worth reading.

On leaving the churchyard, turn left. If you want to see the Saxon coins, call in at the Castle Inn as you pass it. They are displayed on the restaurant wall. But do remember that this is a commercial establishment, not a museum, so it is only right that you should stop for a drink or a meal (their food is highly recommended)

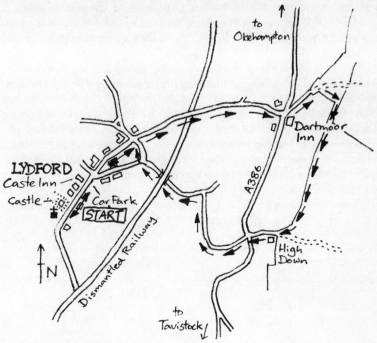

if you do go in.

Continue up the main street of the village until you come to the post office on your right. Just beyond it is a small lane leading off to the right. Go down there and through a gate on your left to see part of the remains of the old Saxon defences.

Return to the street and turn right to leave the village. Follow the road all the way back to the A386. Just across the road is the Dartmoor Inn. This sixteenth-century hostelry features in Charles Kingsley's *Westward Ho!*, in which one Salvation Yeo kills the leader of the Gubbins clan, the outlaws who inhabited Lydford Gorge and preyed on travellers along the western edge of the moor.

Slightly to the left of the pub you will see a track leading half left up towards the moor. Follow it up and through a gate. On the other side, it curves round to reach a car park. Follow it round if you want to stay with the basic route, or go straight on, passing another gate, if you want to go further onto the moor.

Following the basic route, you pass the car park on your left and then go round a gate blocking further vehicular access. Keep to the line of the wall as it goes round to the right. You get very good views, to the left across to Brat Tor and Doe Tor and to the right over farmland, with Brent Tor and its famous church on the horizon half right.

Keep following the wall until you come to a farmhouse. Go to the right of this down a track to a gate. Go through and down to the main road. Cross over to a track on the other side, leading down between hedges. It curves to the right and you eventually come out at a T-junction. Turn left and follow the track, which soon also curves right. This stretch is lined with pink purslane in spring and summer.

The track goes under a dismantled railway line and comes to a junction, with a public footpath going off to the left, a track going straight on and a surfaced lane going right. Turn right to follow the lane. The path, incidentally, is the last stretch of the Lich Path. The whole of Dartmoor Forest was part of Lydford parish, and consequently, until the thirteenth century all the residents of the forest had to be buried in Lydford when they died, even those as far away as Postbridge and Bellever on the eastern side. The Lich Path is the ancient route along which their relatives brought them for burial. (For more on ancient routes, including the Lich Path, see Walk 8.)

Follow the lane until it meets the main street of Lydford at the war memorial, and turn left to return to the car park.

5. Norman Conquerors

OKEHAMPTON CASTLE

THE BACKGROUND

William the Conqueror came to Devon in 1068, and met with some resistance from the Saxons at Exeter. Eventually the city submitted to his authority, but the Saxons continued to harry the Normans with attacks on a number of their manors. Okehampton Castle was probably one of several founded to protect them from these raids.

It is mentioned in the Domesday Book of 1086, and was built, probably soon after William established his hegemony over Devon, by Baldwin de Brionne, Sheriff of the county, who had been granted the Manor of Okehampton, along with nearly 200 others. It was built in a very good defensive position, on a spur of land jutting out into the valley of the West Okement River, with a commanding position over the main ford across the river and next to the road to Cornwall.

Despite its position and its good defences, the castle was never involved in any fighting. In fact, its role probably had more to do with demonstrating the lords' superiority over the locals - initially as Normans, but later simply as aristocrats - than with defending their households. As such, it became not only Baldwin's headquarters and the judicial centre of his estate, but also a symbol of his power and of Norman feudal overlordship. It remained in his family until 1137, when his son Richard died without a male heir. It was subsequently held by the husbands of a succession of female heiresses until 1173, when Hawisia, the last surviving descendant, married Reginald Courtenay, who thus inherited it through her.

The original castle was not very impressive, and probably only comprised the motte and keep, with perhaps a few stone or wooden buildings around them. More substantial buildings were added in the twelfth or early thirteenth century, but it was in the late thirteenth and early fourteenth centuries that the most extensive building took place, and it flourished from then until the sixteenth century.

Life in the castle at this time was lavish. Here the lords dispensed justice, entertained their friends and retainers, and hunted in their large hunting park, which stretched from the river valley all the way south onto Dartmoor. And although none of its owners lived there permanently, even in its heyday, it must have been a bustling place, as it was an important administrative centre, with officials, clerks, servants and others going about their business, whether the lords were in residence or not.

The castle's fortunes reflected those of the family to which it belonged. The Courtenays were extremely powerful, and also held the castles of Tiverton and Plympton. Their downfall, and that of Okehampton Castle, came in 1538, when Henry Courtenay was executed by Henry VIII for treason. His estates were seized by the crown, and the castle was abandoned. It was briefly reoccupied in the late seventeenth century, when parts were altered to accommodate a bakehouse connected with a mill just outside the old walls. By then, however, it was already described as 'decayed'.

A legend associated with the castle concerns Lady Howard of Tavistock, who was said to have poisoned two of her husbands. As a penance, her ghost is forced to travel each night to Okehampton Castle and return with one blade of grass. Only when every blade has been removed will her penance be over.

THE WALK

Start and finish: Meldon Reservoir, south of the A30 near Okehampton. Grid reference 561917

Parking: There is a car park at the reservoir.

Length: 10km (6¼ miles)

Approximate time: The walk itself will take about 3 hours, but you should allow time to explore Okehampton Castle - probably about half an hour.

Degree of difficulty: B

Route summary: I have chosen Meldon Reservoir to start this walk because the approach to Okehampton Castle from this side is not only very attractive, but gives an excellent impression of its imposing position and extensive demesne, and because on the way back you have an opportunity to experience something of the grandeur of these wild northern moors. The route is quite straightforward, but there are several steep climbs, particularly in the latter part of the walk. *Okehampton Castle is an English Heritage property, and is only open from the end of March to the end of October, from 10 a.m. to 6 p.m. There is a small entrance fee. The return part of this walk takes you across Okehampton Range, a military area used for live firing. You should therefore check on firing times before* *setting out. These times are available at Dartmoor Information Centres, local post offices and police stations and are published in the local press. Alternatively, you can telephone Paignton (01803)559782, Exeter (01392) 270164, Plymouth (01752) 501478 or Okehampton (01837) 52939 for recorded information. If there is a red flag flying from the top of Yes Tor when you come out of Okehampton Camp (see the detailed route description below), then firing is taking place and there is no alternative but to retrace your outward route. If there is no flag flying, then it is quite safe to proceed.*

Leave the car park via the small gate just above the toilets. Turn left and immediately left again through a gate (signposted to Meldon Viaduct). Keep to the left of the field as you go down the hill. Where the wall turns left, go half left to a large gap in the wall ahead and follow the path down into the wood. Be careful, as this path can become rather muddy at times.

You cross a small rivulet, and then you will see a footbridge on your right. Cross it and turn left on the other side to follow the other bank of the river. You go through some spoil heaps and soon you will see the rather spectacular Meldon Viaduct, which carries the railway line across the West Okement River, looming up ahead.

Just before the viaduct you come to a gate leading onto a track. Follow the track up to a road, and then follow the road under the viaduct. About 100m beyond the viaduct you will see a sign pointing right saying 'Permitted bridlepath'. Take this path for a delightful amble through the wood which avoids too much road walking. The wood is filled with bluebells and wood sorrel in the spring.

All too soon you rejoin the road. Turn right and follow it round to the left to cross the A30 dual carriageway. Immediately on the other side, take the track leading off to the right (signposted to Okehampton). It leads you through several gates to a farmyard. Turn right through another gate, following the path sign, and turn immediately left to go round the farmyard and rejoin the track on the other side.

At the path junction, go straight on, following the bridlepath sign. You eventually come to a gate which leads onto Okehampton Golf Course. Follow the path across the middle of the golf course, watching out for flying golf balls as you go. As you cross the golf course, you will see Okehampton Castle over to your left. From here you get a very good impression of its imposing situation in relation to what in Norman times would have been its demesnes, with the hunting park stretching across to the right, and of its good defensive position. What you can see from here is only the keep, the main defensive point of the castle; the rest is behind it.

You eventually leave the golf course via a road. Cross a cattle grid and about 250m beyond it, take the path leading half left (signposted to the castle and Okehampton). The full extent of the castle is now visible through the trees on the left. Follow the path down through the wood to the river. Cross the footbridge ahead of you and turn left along the river bank. You will come to a gate on your right; go through it and up the path on the other side. At the top, turn left to reach the castle.

English Heritage provides visitors with a taped commentary to help you as you go around, and it is very useful in explaining its history and capturing something of the atmosphere of the period. Most of the present ruins date from the castle's heyday in the thirteenth and fourteenth centuries, but the first wall you see coming up the slope is original.

Turn right as you leave the castle grounds, and retrace your route back down to the river, through the gate and left to cross the footbridge. On the other side, follow the same path up through the wood (signposted to Meldon Viaduct and Tors Road). At the top of the path, instead of following the road back to the golf course, turn sharp left and follow it in the other direction (signposted to Tors Road).

After about 100m, leave the road and go half right up a path (signposted 'Footpath Tors Road'). It climbs above the road and eventually leads you to a gate onto a road. Go through and turn right. Follow the road up the hill. It curves to the left to cross a railway line. From here you get a very good view across to the castle, again giving you a good impression of its strong defensive position.

The road then crosses the A30 again. Immediately on the other side, turn right down a side road, following the public footpath sign. The road becomes a rough track and bends to the left. At the top, just before it ends at a gate, take the track leading off to the right. This leads to a stile; on the other side you should take the path which branches off the track to the left (signposted to Okehampton Camp).

This path goes up through a wood and out onto open moorland, still climbing. Once out of the wood, you get some quite stunning views behind you and to the right, and you can see the castle again below you. As you come over the brow of the hill, you will see Okehampton Camp in front of you. Make for the gatehouse which lies straight ahead.

Go through the gate and up the road ahead. You may be stopped at the guardroom a little way up the road and given instructions for making your way through the camp, or you may just be waved through. Either way, the route is very clearly marked, both with wooden path signs and with black arrows on a yellow background. Do keep to the public right of way - this is a military establishment and you are therefore not free to wander at will.

You will find that the marked route goes straight up the first road, then left at the top and right at the next T-junction. At the end of the camp, follow the signs to a stile and cross the field on the other side to another stile onto the open moor. You get a superb view out onto the moor here, with three tors looming ahead of you: to the left Row Tor, in the middle West Mill Tor; and to the right and slightly behind West Mill Tor, Yes Tor. It is unlikely that you would have been allowed to get this far through the camp if there is firing on the range, but you should double

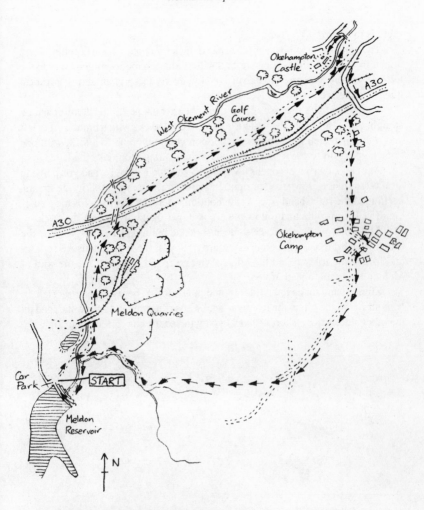

check that there is no red flag flying from Yes Tor.

Follow the track that leads off away from the stile, and where it joins a surfaced road, take the unsurfaced track that goes off to the right. If you have any energy left after your climb up from Okehampton, you might want to climb Yes Tor for some magnificent views, and even go on from there along the fairly easy saddle to High Willhays, the highest point on Dartmoor. But be warned - the climb up to Yes Tor is steep. If you do decide to climb it, then you should follow the surfaced road and leave it as it curves to the left. Contour round West Mill Tor to reach the climb up to Yes Tor. To rejoin the main route from Yes Tor, turn sharp right and make your way down to the valley, then follow the right bank of the brook; if you go on to High Willhays, then the easiest way to rejoin the main route is to return to Yes Tor.

The main route follows the unsurfaced track for about 1.5 km (1 mile). There is an almost eerie stillness up here, and with the barren moors rolling away to the left and behind you and the expansive sky above, there is an almost mystical quality to the scene.

Ignore the track that goes off to the right after about 750m ($^1/_2$ mile) and go straight on. Also ignore the various grass-covered tracks which branch off to left and right; just keep to the main track. Soon you will come to a fork, with one branch going off to the left, and the other going straight on; take the latter.

Another superb view opens up ahead of you and half right, and you come to a valley stretching down to your right. Leave the track here and follow the stream, keeping to the right-hand side. At the bottom, where the stream joins the Red-a-ven Brook, turn right and follow the brook down. You will soon join a track.

At the bottom, you will see some abandoned buildings; bear left to cross the brook via a bridge. On the other side, turn right past the foot of a disused quarry and follow the track round the hill. As you go round, you will see the wall of Meldon Reservoir ahead of you.

Climb round to the left, still following the track. Where it ends, bear right to contour round the hill to the reservoir wall. Cross the wall and follow the road on the other side. After a short distance, you will see the car park on your right.

6. Medieval Villagers

HOUNDTOR MEDIEVAL VILLAGE

THE BACKGROUND

After the climatic changes which brought about the abandonment of many of the Bronze Age settlements in the first millennium BC (see Walk 2), the moor itself appears to have been used mainly for pasturage, although some settlements remained on the fringes, and some seasonal occupation of the higher ground may have continued.

It was not until the Middle Ages that permanent settlements began to be established again on the moor proper, and the so-called medieval village at Hound Tor (which is really no more than a hamlet) gives a very good idea of how they developed. This was the site of a Bronze Age settlement, and some of the remains from that period were incorporated into the medieval village. The site was reoccupied at least as far back as the eighth or ninth century, but the houses were built of turf, so there are no visible remains. It was only in about the thirteenth century that stone began to be used for building again in any quantity.

The people and their livestock lived in the same building, often without even a wall to separate them - although dividing walls were added to some houses later. The cattle were kept in the lower part of the building, below the entrance. At the upper end there were fireplaces, and in some cases cooking pits; the remains of these can still be seen in some of the houses. The walls were up to 2m (6ft) high, with wooden doors, and the roofs were thatched with heather, rushes or straw. This plan, with modifications and improvements, remained the pattern for Devon longhouses for centuries, although obviously the lower part eventually ceased to be used for livestock - indeed, several farmhouses still retain the same basic layout today.

The village must have prospered initially, as there are signs of the addition of extra rooms to some of the houses. But another climatic change, which set in in about the thirteenth century, began to make life difficult for the farmers, as can be seen, for example, in the appearance of corn-drying barns at about this time; the corn could no longer be dried by the sun in the fields, but had to be brought in and dried artificially. It was probably as a result of this change in weather pattern that the village was finally abandoned altogether in the fourteenth or fifteenth century. It was was originally thought that its population was wiped out by the Black Death in the fourteenth century, but some remains have been found dating from after 1350.

THE WALK

Start and finish: Hound Tor. Grid reference 739791
Parking: There is a car park at Hound Tor.
Length: 8.5km (5¼ miles)
Approximate time: 2½ hours
Degree of difficulty: B
Route summary: This is a delightfully varied route, taking in open moorland, beautiful woods and attractive country lanes. It visits Hound Tor medieval village, as well as a medieval farmstead. There is a bit of climbing, some of it moderately steep, but generally the route is fairly easy and straightforward to follow.

Turn left from the car park and follow the road for about 200m until you come to a pull-in on the left. You will see a well-worn path leading off half right to contour round below Hound Tor. After a while, you will cross a bank. This is a medieval wall; it is not as obvious as one might expect because the bracken tends to obscure it, but it is nevertheless quite visible. Follow the track further round, and you will cross another medieval wall. Just beyond it on your left you will see the remains of a farmstead. This is a mixture of medieval and Bronze Age buildings. There are the remains of two Bronze Age huts, one of which was adapted for use as a pen for animals in the Middle Ages, a medieval barn and a medieval longhouse, which has incorporated the remains of a Bronze Age hut into one of its walls.

Continue along the track round Hound Tor, and soon you will see the walls of the medieval village ahead of you, in front and slightly to the left of Greator Rocks. It is interesting to explore the village and try to work out the purpose of the various buildings, but please do not climb on the walls, as they are easily damaged.

The first building you come to is a corn-drying barn; the oven-like constructions at the top end are kilns built to generate the heat needed to dry the crop. There are more such barns further doen the hill to the left. Further into the village are a series of buildings, mainly houses, some quite simple, some more complex. The simplest ones are fairly small and have only one entrance, while at the other end of the scale is a large house with extra rooms leading off the main living area and outhouses built on, all set in its own enclosure. All, however, follow the same basic longhouse pattern of having the livestock below the entrance or entrances, and the human living quarters at the upper end.

From the village, follow the path which leads to the left of Greator Rocks to a gate in the wall. Go through it and down the path on the other side, between a conifer plantation on the left and a field on the right, to another gate. Go through that and continue down the path. As you go down you can see the unmistakable shape of Haytor to your right.

At the bottom, go through another gate and cross the Becka Brook via a stone bridge. This is a lovely area for a picnic. Go up the other side and follow the path through some trees as it winds first to the right and then to the left. It soon emerges from the trees, and as it does so it forks. Take the left fork, which goes up to a signpost. Turn left here, towards Leighon. When you come to a wall round a field, follow the path round to the right and then to the left to circumnavigate it. Do not go round the second field, but follow the path straight on between the two fields. There is a good view left back to Hound Tor and half left to Manaton.

Go through a gate between the two walls and down the path on the other side. Go through a second gate and continue on down. At the end, the path goes to the right and you come to a junction. Go straight on (signposted to Upper Terrace Drive). Go through another gate and up the track on the other side, still with good views over to the left.

The track winds up the hill for about 600m, sticking closely to a wall on the left. As you come out at the top, you get another excellent view half left across woods and farms. When the wall leaves the line of the track and curves away to the left, follow it round to a road. Turn left across a cattle grid and follow the lane on the other side down a hill and through a wood. Cross over a bridge at the bottom, and follow the lane round to the right to join a road. Turn right (signposted to Becky Falls and Bovey Tracey).

After about 100m you will see an entrance on your left, with a 'no parking' sign on the barrier and a public footpath sign beyond it. Go through and turn left to follow the path through a lovely wood alongside a small stream. At the path junction, go left, following the yellow waymarks. Cross a stile and continue along the path, still with the stream on your left. You eventually cross a small footbridge and leave the wood.

Follow the path along the left-hand side of a field. At the end, you join a track, which goes left to take you out onto a road. Turn right. After about 100m, you will see the Kestor Inn on your right and a narrow lane leading off to the left (signposted to Southcott). Turn left here and follow the lane across a stream and up the fairly steep hill on the other side.

After about 600m, you come to a crossroads. Turn left. You pass a lovely old stone farmhouse on your right, and soon afterwards the lane curves round to the right. As you follow it round, you should get a good view across to Haytor Down on your left, with Greator Rocks half left and Hound Tor just coming into view up ahead. You pass another lovely old farmhouse on your right and the lane goes sharply to the left. At the T-junction up ahead, go right (signposted to Widecombe). The lane climbs and winds and eventually crosses a cattle grid onto the open moor. About 500m beyond the cattle grid, you will see the car park on your right.

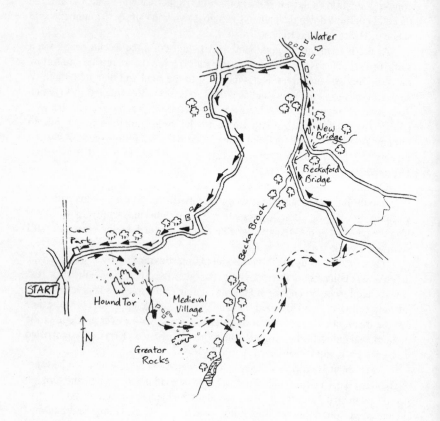

——— 7. Tenant Farmers and Ancient Rights ———

JUDGE'S CHAIR, DUNNABRIDGE POUND

——————— THE BACKGROUND ———————

Dartmoor Forest covers most of the central area of the National Park. This does not mean that it was once covered in trees; the word 'forest' originally meant simply a royal hunting ground, whether it was wooded or not. Indeed almost all of Devon was once a royal forest, and subject to severe forest laws. These laws were aimed at protecting deer, hares, boars and wolves for the royal hunt. But in 1204, most of the county was deforested, leaving only Dartmoor and Exmoor, which belonged to the king. In 1239 Henry III gave Dartmoor to Richard, Earl of Cornwall. Edward III made his son, the Black Prince, Duke of Cornwall and the Forest has belonged to the Duchy of Cornwall ever since. The present Duke of Cornwall is, of course, Prince Charles.

Within the Forest were 35 holdings called ancient tenements, including Pizwell and Dunnabridge. They were held by what was called copyhold; there was no evidence of their ownership except a copy of the entry in the roll of the manor court. But the tenants' rights had been held 'since ancient times', hence the name of their holdings.

The tenants owed various obligations to the lord of the manor (i.e. the Duke). The most important, of course, was to obey the forest laws and do nothing to injure or disturb the game or its cover, which must have made farming very difficult. Their duties also included attending manorial courts at Lydford, having their corn ground at the Duke's mill at Babeny and assisting at regular drifts. These drifts involved rounding up cattle and horses which were grazing in the forest without authorisation and taking them to drift pounds, of which

Dunnabridge Pound was the most important. Their owners then had three weeks in which to pay a fee to have them released, otherwise the stock were sold by auction.

The experts are not sure how old Dunnabridge Pound is, but it almost certainly predates the Middle Ages - although it is probably not prehistoric. Within it can be seen a large stone called the Judge's Chair. It is not clear what its origin is. It was at one time thought that it was the judge's seat from Crockern Tor, but that appears unlikely. Other suggestions are that it was an ancient burial chamber and that it is the remains of the stocks which were used for anyone who disrupted proceedings at the pound.

In addition to their duties, the holders of the ancient tenements also had certain privileges, including the right to free pasturage in the forest and the right to take turf, fuel or stones from it. On taking over a tenement, an heir or a new tenant also had the right to enclose a 'newtake' of 8 acres for his own use up to 1796, when the practice ceased.

THE WALK

Start and finish: Postbridge. Grid reference 647789
Parking: In the car park at Postbridge
Length: 9.75km (6 miles)
Approximate time: $2^1/_2$ -3 hours
Degree of difficulty: B
Links with: Walk 16
Route summary: Although it is quite long, this is not a difficult walk. There are few climbs of any significance, and the route is easy to follow. It combines some very pleasant forest tracks, a stretch of open moorland, farm paths and a riverside amble, with some superb viewpoints. It takes you to Dunnabridge and the pound, and returns via Pizwell.

Turn right from the car park and take the road almost immediately on your left, across a cattle grid (signposted to Bellever). On the other side, turn right into Bellever Forest and immediately left up a track to a gate with a public footpath sign. Go through the gate and follow the track through the trees and across a clearing. Ignore the track going off to the right and carry straight on up the hill (signposted to Bellever and Tor).

At the top, look back for a superb view across the rolling moors. Where the track forks, go right (signposted to Bellever Tor). About 800m ($^1/_2$ mile) further on, you come to another junction. The path at right angles to the one you are on is the Lich Path or Lichway, and is the ancient route once used by people from the eastern side of Dartmoor Forest as they took their dead to be buried at Lydford (for more on this ancient track, see Walk 8).

Cross the Lich Path and follow the path ahead (signposted to Dunnabridge Pound). You finally leave the trees and cross a wall, from where you will see

Bellever Tor up ahead of you. Take the broad grassy track up the tor for some fantastic views - if you actually climb the rocks at the top, you get a 360-degree panorama. You can skirt round to the left, following the line of the trees, to avoid the climb, but the view is well worth the small extra effort.

Follow the clear path down through the gorse on the other side of the tor to a wall. When you reach it, go through the gate in the corner on the left, not across the stile. Follow the wall on your right all the way down to another gate. Go through and continue along the wall until it turns sharply to the right. Instead of following it round, go half right to cut off the corner and you will come out at a gate, with Dunnabridge Pound on your left. If you look across to the gate leading towards the road, you will see the Judge's Chair alongside it. You should not enter the pound, however, as it is private property.

Turn sharp left along a track (signposted at the gate to Laughter Hole Farm). Follow the track to a gate, and then on to a gap in a dilapidated wall. There are still good views behind you and to your right, and now also ahead of you. The track leads you to another gate, with a signpost pointing to Bellever. Go through and, ignoring the track leading off to the left, carry straight on down a hill, following the path sign.

At the bottom, go straight on (signposted to Bellever) and through yet another gate. The track now takes you past some trees and then a cleared area, back into Bellever Forest. Ignore the turning to the right just before you enter the trees, but as the track bends to the left go straight on through a gate.

You pass some toilets on your left, and then leave the forest and come to a road. Turn right and follow the road to Bellever Bridge. Just to the right of the main bridge you will see the remains of an old clapper bridge. The central span is missing, and it is thought that this may have been made of wood rather than stone.

Cross the bridge, and after a few yards you will see a path leading off to the left, following a little stream. Follow this path upstream for about 600m until you come to a track. Turn right and you will soon come to a stile on your left, with a sign indicating that it is a permitted footpath to Pizwell. Turn left here and cross the stile. Follow the grassy track on the other side. At the end of the field, go right and then left, following the path signs. You are now on a very much more definite track. After another 200m or so, you will come to a junction, with another track going off to the left (signposted to Postbridge).

Pizwell Farm is straight ahead, and the track is a public right of way, but the route of the walk turns left to follow the track down to cross a stream. The stream flows along the track for a short distance, so you will either have to keep to the grass alongside it or do a bit of wading - it is only an inch or two deep, so it is not much of a problem.

Go through a gate on the other side and continue along the track. Follow it round to the left following the bridlepath sign, and through another gate. Keep to the right of the field beyond alongside a wall and fence. You will come to a bank

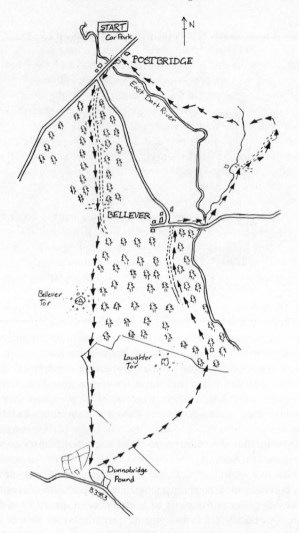

topped with gorse. Turn left, and at the bottom right, following the direction of the path signs. Go through a gate and cross a field to another gate. Go through and you will find the river about 50m down on your left.

You finally come out, via another gate, at the Lydgate House Hotel. Pass the hotel and follow the drive out of the gate. Just beyond the gate, you will see a kissing gate on your left, with a sign pointing to a permitted path to the clapper bridge. Turn left down here and follow the path across two footbridges and through a gate. Postbridge's famous clapper bridge is ahead of you. This bridge is at least 500 years old, although it has obviously been restored. Cross the clapper bridge and join the road on the other side. Turn left to return to the car park.

8. Travellers of Yore

ROUTE MARKER, TER HILL

THE WALK

Roads were not really established on Dartmoor until the eighteenth century. Before that there were only tracks, and the rough terrain was not conducive to wheeled traffic, so goods were transported mainly by packhorse and sledge. In some places, because of the nature of the land, travellers were restricted to a narrow route and the track was quite clear. In others, where the going was easier, they could spread out and the route was not so obvious. Where it was difficult to follow, markers (often crosses) were erected to show the way. Many of these ancient routes can still be followed today, either because the track is well trodden or because some of the markers remain.

William Crossing, in his *Guide to Dartmoor*, lists 81 'principal' tracks and paths, but many of these are just local routes to particular places for particular purposes: to gather turf or reeds, to reach a mine or quarry, or to drive cattle to pasture. Others cross the moor from one end to the other. Most of the routes are unnamed, but some of the major ones have names which describe their main purpose: the Jobbers' Road (used by wool jobbers collecting wool from the farms along the way), the Mariners' Way (used by sailors travelling from Bideford to join ships in Dartmouth and vice versa), the Lich Path (used by people carrying their dead for burial at Lydford), Black Lane (used for the transport of peat) and the Monks' Path (which linked the abbeys of Buckfast and Tavistock). Of course, many of them probably existed before they were used for the purposes which gave them their names, and only later became associated with particular traffic.

It may seem strange today that people should choose to cross the exposed moor, with its mists and its mires, rather than using more 'civilised' routes around

37

the edge. But in the Middle Ages, the lanes of what was called the 'in country' - the enclosed land surrounding the moor - were often extremely muddy and difficult to negotiate. At least on the open moor, travellers could usually avoid the worst areas by going round them, but in the surrounding country, hedges kept them to the lane.

The Lich Path has an interesting history. Dartmoor Forest formed part of Lydford parish, and since it was a requirement of the Church that when anyone died they should be buried in their parish churchyard, people had to carry their dead all the way from as far east as Postbridge and Bellever for burial - a distance of 11$^{1}/_{2}$ miles, or 18$^{1}/_{2}$ miles in bad weather. In 1260, however, Bishop Branscombe of Exeter agreed that those on the eastern edge of the Forest could use Widecombe Church. Since that time, the Lich Path ceased to be used for its original purpose, although it continued to be used as a general transmoor route.

The Jobbers' Road probably dates from the thirteenth century, or perhaps even earlier. The wool industry flourished on Dartmoor from about 1350 to 1500. The jobbers collected fleeces and yarn from the farms along the southern edge of the moor and took them to Sheepstor, in the south-western corner, which was an important centre for the the wool trade. This road is now usually, but almost certainly mistakenly, called the Abbot's Way, even on Ordnance Survey maps. The implication behind the name is that it was the route (or one of the routes) linking Buckfast and Tavistock abbeys. However, it is not the easiest route across the moor for travellers on foot; the Monks' Path, further north is considerably easier. Moreover, if it were the route between the two abbeys, one would expect it to be marked by crosses, which it is not. Whereas the wool jobbers and farmers would have known the moor intimately, the monks at the two abbeys would have come from all over the country, and would therefore need markers of some kind to show them the way.

THE WALK

Start and finish: Cross Furzes, near Buckfastleigh. Grid reference 700666. (Note: The Ordnance Survey map is somewhat confusing; The walk does not start at the road junction where the name 'Cross Furzes' appears, but at the junction 200m south-east of it, where the road from Hockmoor Head on the Buckfast-Holne road meets the Buckfastleigh-Scorriton road.)

Parking: There is a small pull-in at the side of the road.

Length: 21km (13 miles)

Approximate time: 6 hours

Degree of difficulty: C

Links with: Walk 18

Route summary: This is a magnificent moorland hike. The views are outstanding and there is a marvellous feeling of space and freedom. It takes you out along the Jobbers' Road, then joins an unnamed north-south ancient route to return via the Monks' Path. It is not a walk to be undertaken in poor visibility, however, unless you have the requisite navigational skills; there are few major landmarks and the paths are not always clearly defined. The going is also rather difficult at times (though never excessively so).

Cross the road at the T-junction and follow the track on the other side (signposted to Plym Ford and Nun's Cross for Princetown and also to Moor Gate for South Brent). The track leads you down to a stream, where you cross a stone bridge beside a ford. Go through the gate on the other side and then straight on (signposted to Plym Ford and Nun's Cross for Princetown). The path is fairly obvious as it winds up the hill on the other side, and it is clearly marked with signs and waymarks. As you go look back for a very good view over farms and woods. You are now on the Jobbers' Road, although it is now almost universally known as the Abbot's Way.

About 800m (¹/₂ mile) after crossing the stream, you come to a bank. Shortly after crossing the bank, bear right to a gate in the fence ahead. Continue along the clear path beyond the gate, and when you come to a stream, go right to cross it. As you climb up the other side, you get a good view across the moors ahead of you. Follow the waymarks along a fence on the right to a gate out onto the moor.

Bear left beyond the gate to follow the line of a fence on your left for a short way. Where it turns left, however, go straight on up the hill. As you come over the brow of the hill, you will see the strange submarine-like shape of Eastern White Barrow on the horizon ahead. This is a Bronze Age burial site, but why it is has been given such a strange form is a mystery. This was certainly not its original shape; it has been rebuilt comparatively recently, although no one seems to know why.

You will soon see the Avon Dam over on your left. Keep following the track as it goes down the hill to the right of the dam to cross a stream at the bottom. On the other side the track skirts round to the left. If you look to your right as you go round, you will see the remains of a Bronze Age settlement above you, consisting of a walled enclosure and some huts (for more on Bronze Age settlements, see Walk 2).

The track is still quite clear as you go round the hill, with the long arm of the Avon Dam on your left. After a while, the pyramid-shaped spoil tip of the Red Lake china clay quarry (see Walk 18) comes into view in the distance. Towards the head of the dam, the track narrows to a path, but it is still quite clear as it follows the valley of the River Avon.

You will come to a stream crossing your path. Cross it and continue to follow the Avon on the other side. The area up the hill on your right is Huntingdon Warren, where rabbits were once 'farmed'; from time to time you will see the buries that were constructed for the rabbits to burrow in (for more on warrening, see Walk 11).

Keep following the path round the hill until you see a stone footbridge across the river to your left. Cross here and climb the hill on the other side. It does not much matter how you negotiate the hill: you can take the direct but steep route or follow the barely discernible path that goes to the left and then later to the right to avoid the worst of the climbing. The main thing is not to cross the gully beyond the hill, but to turn to the right and go almost due east along the top of it.

It is beautifully tranquil up here. There is nothing but the empty moorland stretching away apparently endlessly in every direction and the enormous expanse of the sky above you. And the silence is usually broken only by the occasional bird call. As you crest the hill, you will see the spoil heap at Red Lake again, this time on your right. You pass a disused shed on your left. Soon you will see a clear track leading away from you. It is the disused line of the railway which served the china clay works, and you should aim for it.

When you reach it, follow it for a short distance, but when you come to the ruins of a building on your right, bear right to contour round the hill along a grassy track which then follows the Red Lake stream down its shallow valley. Find a convenient place to cross the stream and continue to follow it on the other side. After a while, you will find that Red Lake veers left away from the path to join the River Erme. Continue along the path, which climbs above the stream and then crosses a stone row - but not just an ordinary stone row. This is the longest ancient stone row in Britain, stretching for 3.5km ($2^{1}/_{2}$ miles) from the stone circle known as the Dancers on Stall Moor to a burial chamber on Green Hill (for more on stone rows, see Walk 1).

As you come over the hill, you will see the River Erme flowing towards you up ahead. Go down and follow it up. Cross a stream and then bear right to leave the Jobbers' Road and join an unnamed north-south trans-Dartmoor route which linked Okehampton with the South Hams. This route was probably used mainly by local farmers on their way to the markets on the edge of the moor rather than as a transmoor route like the Jobbers' Road. It is also not a definite track in the way that the Jobbers' Road has been for most of the walk so far; here on the open moor there was no need to keep to a specific track, and it was the general direction between certain points that defined the route.

There is therefore no clear track up here, although you will come across a path of sorts from time to time. However, as you come over the hill, you will see the Blacklane Brook on your left, and your route follows the line of the brook, so as long as you keep it in view to your left you can pick your own way. The going is easy at first, but about 800m ($^{1}/_{2}$ mile) after leaving the Jobbers' Road, you will pass the spoil heaps of some old tin workings, and after that it becomes more difficult, with tussocks of grass. About 200m beyond the spoil heaps, you pass a wooden post on your left.

You follow the Blacklane Brook for a total of about 2.5km ($1^{1}/_{2}$ miles). Higher up, there are one or two marshy stretches which should be crossed with care - you may need to go up to your right to find a suitable crossing place. And as you go higher up the valley the brook becomes less and less obvious, until near the top it is little more than a narrow channel. Nevertheless, as long as you do not stray too far from it, you should be able to follow its line without difficulty.

At the head of the brook, you come to another wooden post, to the left of which is a gully leading away from you. This is called Black Lane, and is an old peat-cutters' track. You get a very good view up ahead, with the television mast on North Hessary Tor clearly visible half left and Beardown Tors and Longaford Tor directly ahead. As you round a corner you will see the rocks of Fox Tor immediately in front of you.

As you go towards Fox Tor, you will pass into an abandoned tin working called a girt (for more on tin mining, see Walk 10). Follow it down until it meets another girt, which crosses it at right angles. Turn right and follow the new girt down alongside a stream. You are now leaving the north-south route to cut across and join the third of our routes, the Monks' Path.

Keep to the right of the stream, and stretching up the hill across the valley ahead, you will see a wall. Aim for that, leaving the valley and cutting up to the slightly higher ground. As you come over the hill, you will see the rest of the wall. Aim for the bottom corner. Pick your way down to a stream - the slope is quite steep, but some routes are easier than others. Cross the stream and make your way to the wall. Go round the corner and follow the wall up the hill. As you go, you will find a very pleasant view over to your left.

At the top of the wall, you will see a cross in the corner of the field on your left. This tells you that you have now joined the Monks' Path, as it is one of a string of crosses that once marked that route, of which only a few now remain. Turn right and make your way across the moor. After a few yards, you will see the top of another cross peeping above the horizon; make for that. When you reach it, turn half left to a third cross which you can see a short distance away. The views from here are magnificent.

The Monks' Path goes straight on here, but we need to turn right. There is no path, but as you come over the hill, you will see the big gash of Skir Gut ahead. Aim to the right of that, to skirt round the top of it. When you get to Skir Gut, carry straight on. On a clear day, you should be able to see the triangulation pillar on top of Ryder's Hill on the horizon ahead of you. If you cannot see it, just keep walking in a straight line towards the highest point on the ridge. If you are walking with a compass, the bearing is 138. The terrain on this stretch is a bit rough and there are several dips, but it is quite manageable.

As you cross the valley towards Ryder's Hill, you will come to Aune Head Mires. This is a very boggy area, and you will have to negotiate it with care - you may need to swing to the left to find the best way around it. Once past it, make your way up Ryder's Hill, still trying to aim for the highest point. You will not be able to see the triangulation pillar from here, but once you get to the ridge it should be clearly visible and you can make your way to it. The views from up here are quite spectacular - the tremendous rolling expanse of the high moorland to the north, and lush green farmland to the east.

From the trig point you will see the cairn on the top of Snowdon across the

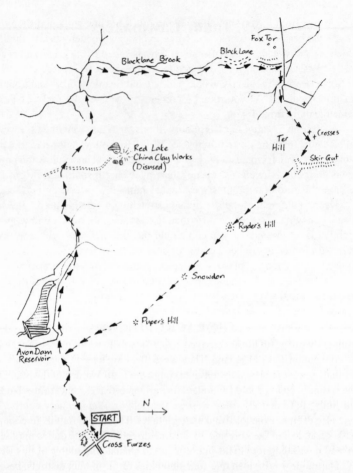

dip ahead of you. Follow the grassy track which leads up to it. When you get to Snowdon, you will see that there are in fact two cairns, both Bronze Age burial chambers. Turn half right and you will see another cairn on the top of the next hill, Pupers Hill. Aim for that. cross some old tin workings and follow the grassy track across the dip to it.

From there, bear left along another grassy track. Another superb view appears ahead of you and soon also to the left. Cross another track and carry on. You will find a low bank on your right - the remains of a Bronze Age reave or boundary work (see Walk 2). You then cross a stream. A little way beyond the stream, the track becomes rather indistinct, but you should keep going straight on, aiming for a small clump of trees. When you reach them, turn left. You are now back on the Jobbers' Road. Go left down to the gate and retrace your route, following the signs and waymarks across the fields and up the track, back to Cross Furzes.

9. Tudor Lawmakers

CROCKERN TOR

THE BACKGROUND

From early times, tin miners enjoyed a significant degree of independence from the civil authorities of England. They were 'the king's men', and in many areas of life they were subject only to him through the Lord Warden of the Stannaries. The ordinary courts could try tinners for serious offences concerning 'land, life and limb', but otherwise they were subject only to the stannary courts. They were also exempt from local and national taxes. The reason for this freedom was that a great deal of the king's income came directly from the duties imposed on tin, and it was therefore in his interests not to alienate the source of this wealth.

Dartmoor was divided into four stannaries or tin-mining districts, based on Chagford, Tavistock, Ashburton and Plympton. Originally, representatives of the miners of both Devon and Cornwall met in Cornwall to make and amend the laws relating to the industry, including the registration of claims, the regulation of smelting and the criteria for deciding who could have an interest in tin works, and to fix the penalties for contravening the tinners' ancient rights. Later, the Devon miners held their own assembly called the Great Court, which met at Crockern Tor, where the boundaries of the four stannaries met. Slabs of rock, many of them now removed, served as seats and tables. The Lord Warden or Vice-Warden may have sat on one of the steps of Parliament Rock or on a special seat since removed, with the clerks and the miners' representatives, called stannators or jurates, on the grass or rocks below him.

The first records of the Great Court date from 1494, but it probably existed for some time before then - perhaps even as early as the beginning of the fourteenth century. Assemblies were called whenever the Lord Warden thought necessary; tinners in each stannary elected 24 stannators - an extremely democratic system for its time.

The tinners' favoured position caused a great deal of resentment among the ordinary citizenry of the area, particularly as they all too often abused their privileges. For example, they had the right to dig for tin wherever they chose (landowners did not have the mineral rights to their land), and this often led them to destroy farmland, woods and even homes and gardens with impunity. They often resisted arrest by the civil authorities. Even when they were found guilty of an offence, they could only be imprisoned in their own prison at Lydford Castle, and they were sometimes freed by their fellow tinners.

Moreover, at the height of their powers, the stannary courts did not confine themselves to matters relating to tin mining. They tended to hear any case where a tinner was involved, regardless of the cause. Since the cases were decided by a jury of tinners, this meant that a non-tinner had little chance of obtaining justice if he was in dispute with a tinner. And anyone who tried to curb their behaviour risked being accused (in the stannary courts, of course) of seeking to infringe their ancient rights. This is what happened to Richard Strode MP in 1512 when he tried to introduce a law at Westminster restricting mining near Devon's ports. The law failed, and he was tried by the stannary courts and fined. When he refused to pay, he was imprisoned at Lydford Castle for three weeks.

Strode's treatment, however, marked the peak of the stannary courts' influence. After that, partly because of his efforts, their powers were gradually reduced. The Great Court also began to meet less and less frequently, and stopped altogether in the eighteenth century. By then, in any case, it was the custom to open its sessions at Crockern Tor and then adjourn to the relative comfort of Tavistock - a sensible idea given Crockern Tor's bleak and exposed situation!

THE WALK

Start and finish: Two Bridges. Grid reference 609750
Parking: There is a small parking area opposite the Two Bridges Hotel.
Length: 7.5km (4¹/₂ miles)
Approximate time: 2 hours
Degree of difficulty: A/B
Links with: Walk 16
Route summary: This is a beautiful moorland ramble, taking in some outstanding views and one lovely stretch of woodland, and with several interesting features to see along the way. The route mostly follows well-defined paths, and even where it does go across open moorland, there are clear landmarks to guide you. Apart from one short climb up to Crockern Tor, it is also very easy going.

Turn left along the road from the parking area, in the direction of Dartmeet. At the junction, go left (signposted to Postbridge, Moretonhampstead and Exeter).

As you go, you get a good view to the right, and you can see Crockern Tor ahead of you and Littaford Tors and Longaford Tor to the left.

About 700m after the road junction, you will pass a house on your left called Parson's Cottage. Just beyond it there is a ladder stile on the left, marked 'Footpath'. Cross it (or go through the gate a few yards further on) and climb the short distance to Crockern Tor. The most prominent rock on the tor is the Parliament Rock, on the steps of which the Lord Warden is believed to have sat during sessions of the Great Court. If you climb to the highest point of the tor, the views on a clear day are superb in almost every direction. However, with the wind blowing and the mist swirling round it, it must have presented a bleak prospect, even to the hardy tinners.

Look ahead of you to the north from Crockern Tor, and you will see the large bulk of Longaford Tor sticking up over the horizon. Aim for that, walking parallel to the valley of the West Dart on your left. As you come over the brow of the hill, you will see the smaller outcrops of Littaford Tors in front of Longaford Tor, and a wall running across your route and down to the right. Make for the corner of the wall, where there is a ladder stile. Cross it and make your way to Littaford Tors. The views from here are again quite superb, especially from the further of the two outcrops of rock where you have a 360-degree panorama.

Bear left from Littaford Tors across the rough grass, and as you go down the hill you will see a copse below you. Aim for that, but skirt round to the right of it and make your way down to the wall at the bottom of the hill. Keep to the path which runs slightly above the wall, as the lower stretches tend to be rather marshy.

You will see a green hut on the opposite side of the river, and immediately opposite it a ladder stile across the wall. Cross the stile to a weir across the West Dart River, and cross the river either at the weir or at the rocks above or below it. This is the beginning of the Devonport Leat, a 43km (27-mile) waterway built at the end of the eighteenth century to supply water to Devonport, now part of Plymouth (see Walk 12).

Turn left to follow the leat, keeping to the well-worn path along the left-hand bank. Alternatively, you can climb up to Beardown Tors for more magnificent views. Do not worry if there is a red flag flying from Beardown Tors; this is to warn you that there is firing beyond the tors. Beardown Tors themselves are not in the military range, and provided you do not venture further to the west of them, you will be safe.

If you do climb Beardown Tors, bear left at the top and go down to a gate. Go through it and make your way down the slope to join the leat. Make sure that you cross to the left bank, otherwise you will find your way blocked by a fence as the leat enters the plantation lower down.

If you are not climbing Beardown Tors, follow the leat as it contours round the hill, with the river cascading down the valley on your left. As you go round the hill, you will see Wistman's Wood on the slope opposite. This is an ancient oak wood, but although the trees are very old, none is more than about 5m (15ft) high.

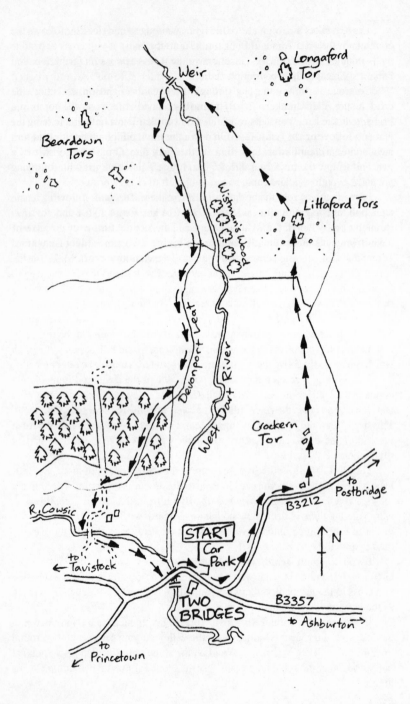

The leat takes you high above the river, winding in and out as it follows the contours of the hill. About 2km ($1^1/_2$ miles) after joining it you cross two stone walls in quick succession by a bridge over the leat. A few yards further on, you cross a stile and enter a conifer plantation.

Continue to follow the leat through the plantation and on the other side cross a stile, then another. Shortly after this second stile, you will come to a bridge over the leat, with a gate and a stile on your left. Turn left here, leaving the leat and following the path sign. Go down the track on the other side and turn right at the farm buildings, following another path sign. Cross another stile by a gate and follow the track round to the left. At the T-junction go right, following yet another path sign and curve round to the left to cross a bridge.

Immediately across the bridge, turn left off the track, again following a path sign, and take the path alongside the River Cowsic. Cross a stile and continue through a pretty wood. Cross another stile and then a little further on go up some steps, over yet another stile and across a footbridge. Two more stiles take you out to a road. Turn left and follow the road back to the parking area.

10. Tinners Over the Centuries

MORTAR-STONES AND MOULD, GOBBET MINE

THE BACKGROUND

Although Cornish tin is known to have been exported in ancient times, it is not known when it was first mined in Devon. There is evidence of tinning in the twelfth century, but the first written reference, in 1198, implies that the industry was already well established by then.

The earliest method of obtaining the ore was by streaming, which, as the term implies, involved shovelling and panning it from the beds of streams. This practice continued until the seventeenth century, and even later in some areas. However, as the deposits in the valley bottoms were exhausted, the tinners started to work the lodes on either side, digging out the ore with picks and shovels. Where possible, leats were built, sometimes from nearby rivers and sometimes from specially constructed rainwater pools, to carry water through the workings and wash away the waste. Mining was very much a small-scale affair, with individual tinners or small groups working their claims.

For centuries, the bulk of Dartmoor tin was extracted in this way - dug from open trenches and pits. The miners could not dig too deep, as they had no way at that time of pumping out the water which would accumulate. In any case, there was still enough ore near to the surface to make deeper mining unnecessary. The remains of many of these workings can still be seen, in the form of girts (deep gullies where the ore was excavated) and spoil heaps.

Once extracted, the small stones of ore were ground between two mill stones. Later, with the introduction of the water-powered knacking mill, which worked like a pestle and mortar, larger stones could be broken up before being ground. The ore was then smelted. Originally, it had two smeltings; the first was done on site and gave a very low-grade, gritty metal, and the second was usually done in one of the stannary towns under the supervision of a royal official. The fourteenth century saw the introduction of blowing houses, which produced a much better-quality metal at the first smelting and obviated the need for a second. They were built of stone and turf, with thatched roofs. A waterwheel powered a set of bellows to get the furnace up to the right temperature, and the molten tin flowed into a stone float, from which it was ladled into moulds.

As the easily accessible ore was worked out, tinning became less and less economical. Mining ceased during the Civil War, although it restarted in a smaller way soon afterwards. It stopped again in the early eighteenth century, but the increased demand generated by the Industrial Revolution, combined with the new technology which was now available, made it a viable undertaking once more towards the end of the century, although production levels were generally lower than in medieval times, and more sporadic.

This was a very different industry from the small-scale operations of the Middle Ages, not only in terms of production levels. The development of new pumping and hoisting gear made underground mining possible, while the cost of that gear ensured that independent tinners could not compete. This then was the era of the mining companies, often with quite large holdings.

The new mines were, of course, very often established on the sites of medieval workings. Hooten Wheals, the Henroost and the Gobbet Mine all show signs of medieval production. At the Gobbet Mine there are mortar stones (used for the initial crushing), milling stones (for the second crushing) and moulds. All that remains of Hooten Wheals are the dressing floors, where the crushed ore was separated from the waste, and the buddles, which were used for washing the ore. The rest of the buildings were badly damaged in military exercises during the Second World War and destroyed. And at the Henroost, only the workings themselves remain.

The Gobbet Mine ceased operations in 1890, but Hooten Wheals continued production until 1920, when a storm caused severe flooding of the workings. Although there were proposals for reopening the mine in 1925, nothing came of them. Indeed, the whole industry on Dartmoor went into a decline at this time in the face of competition from abroad, especially Malaya.

THE WALK

Start and finish: Just west of Hexworthy. Grid reference 650727
Parking: Just east of Hexworthy on the road to Holne, there is a turn-off to the west, signposted to Sherberton. Turn up there and at the moor gate at the end there is a small parking area on the right.
Length: 7km (4¼ miles)
Approximate time: 2 hours
Degree of difficulty: A/B
Route summary: This is a short and fairly easy walk, with little climbing and with just one short stretch in the middle where you are without a path or a clear landmark nearby. It nevertheless gives you a real taste of the open moor, as well as a chance to see the remains of the tin miners' activities over the centuries.

Go back along the road, away from the moor gate. After about 100m, turn right down a track to a gate. Go through and follow the wall on your left. As you go, you get extensive views to your right and behind you.

Where the wall turns to the left, follow it round. After about 500m, look to your right and you will see the remains of a stone circle (for more on stone circles, see Walk 1). Ignore the grassy track going off half right about 600m beyond the stone circle, and continue along the wall for another 600m or so. You will begin to descend steeply to the valley of the strangely named O Brook, crossing a dry leat as you do so.

Turn right at the bottom of the valley and follow the brook. As you go, especially as you get higher up the valley, you will come across a number of mounds. These are the spoil tips from the activities of the earliest tinners, those who obtained the ore by streaming. Be careful in the higher reaches of the valley, as the ground near the brook can be rather marshy; you may need to veer off to the right occasionally, away from the brook, to avoid the worst areas.

After following the brook for about 1km (just over $\frac{1}{2}$ mile), you will see the much larger spoil tips of Hooten Wheals half left. Find a convenient place to cross and make you way up towards them. As you do so you will see the remains of the dressing floors, and below them the circular biddles.

Carry on up to the top, then turn right down a gully. This is a girt, the remains of the second stage in the evolution of tinning, when there was not enough ore left in the streams and the miners began to dig up from the valleys following the lines of the lodes. You can see that it slopes down to the valley floor so that any water drained out.

At the bottom you come to a track. Turn left and follow the track up the valley past a stone bridge on your right. When it bears left away from the brook, follow it. If you look carefully over to your right as you go up, you will see a cross in the middle of the moor on the other side of the brook. This is one of the crosses that marked the route of the Monks' Path (for more on ancient tracks, see Walk 8). The track peters out at the remains of the Henroost mine. All that is left is some deep pits, but the girts round about are an indication that this was the site of mining in the Middle Ages.

From the Henroost, you have to make your way across the open moor, with few landmarks for a while. Bear slightly right from the direction of the track you have just left. On a clear day, you should be able to see the mast on North Hessary Tor, above Princetown, on the far horizon. Aim to the right of that. (If you are walking with a compass, the bearing is about 315.) Do not worry if you go too far to the right, as you can always correct your route later. You cross the O Brook, which here is little more than a narrow channel. The going is a bit rough, and it can be a little marshy, but it is not too difficult. If the visibility is good, you will see another of the crosses marking the route of the Monks' Path on the horizon to your left.

This short stretch is typical of this part of the moor, with gently rolling hills

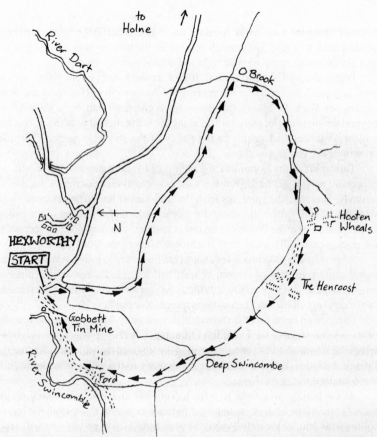

rather than steep tors, and lovely cloud effects in the expansive sky above you. After about 700m, you will come to Deep Swincombe, a valley running down half right. If you find at this stage that you have veered too far from the route, this is the time to correct your direction. Keep to the right of the valley and follow it down. You will come to a wall; go to the left of it, alongside the stream.

You will soon come to another wall across your path. Cross it, and then a stile over a fence, and follow the path which bears right across the field to a gap in the next wall. Go straight down to a track at the bottom of the hill. Turn right, and follow the track along the valley floor, ignoring the footbridge on your left.

The track curves to the right away from the river. When it curves right again and goes into a slight dip, go down to the left. Here you will find the stones from the old blowing house. At the top of the hollow you will see one of the milling stones and at the bottom the other. In between are mortar stones and mould stones.

Continue along the track. Go round the gate at the end and turn right at the road. Follow the road up the hill and cross a cattle grid alongside the moor gate to return to the parking area.

11. 300 Years of Warrening

KENNEL FIELD, DITSWORTHY WARREN

THE BACKGROUND

Rabbits are believed to have been introduced to Britain by the Normans, and on Dartmoor they were extensively farmed in specially constructed warrens from the seventeenth century, perhaps even earlier.

These warrens were usually established in wide areas, wherever possible bounded by rivers, as these formed natural boundaries. In the absence of rivers, walls had to be built to enclose them. Special artificial mounds called buries were created to encourage the rabbits to burrow. They were made of rock, earth and turf, and were surrounded by drainage ditches to provide the dry conditions rabbits prefer. Entrance holes were made get them started.

The 'harvesting' of the rabbits was done in the winter. The warrener would place nets over the entrance holes while the rabbits were feeding and then let his dogs loose. They would chase the rabbits, which naturally headed for home, only to be caught in the nets. Gin traps and ferrets were also used. The meat was sold in the local towns, and the skins were sent to furriers.

Stoats, weasels and other predators were a problem for the warreners, and they would set vermin traps along their runs to catch them. These had floors, sides and roofs of granite, with slate doors at the ends, which dropped when activated by trip wires in the trap. There were walls at each end to funnel the animals into the trap. The warrener would then kill them and sell their skins. These traps fell into disuse in the nineteenth century, when shotguns began to be used for vermin control.

Ditsworthy was the last commercial warren on Dartmoor, and did not cease operations until the 1940s. Some of its buries remain, however, and also the stone kennels in which the warrener's dogs were once kept (they were later provided with warmer and healthier wooden kennels).

THE WALK

Start and finish: Cadover Bridge. Grid reference 555646
Parking: There is a car park on the southern side of Cadover Bridge.
Length: 9.25km (5³/₄ miles)
Approximate time: 2¹/₂ hours
Degree of difficulty: B
Route summary: This moderately long but easy amble takes you across three of Dartmoor's many warrens. It offers lovely moorland walking, with some very good views but few climbs and little rough ground to bother you.

From the car park turn left into the road, and almost immediately right just before the bridge onto another road. Follow it as it winds up the valley of the River Plym, with the Shaugh Lake china clay works clearly visible on your right. You will see two small tracks on your left and then, just as the road bends to the right, a third, more well-defined one also on your left. Turn off here.

The track crosses the Blacka Brook and then winds up towards Trowlesworthy Warren Farm. It curves round to the left of the farm buildings; just before the farm gate, branch left to pass the buildings. As you come round, you will see Great Trowlesworthy Tor ahead of you. Aim towards the left-hand end of the hill leading up to it.

Cross a rather muddy rivulet and you should be able to see a distinct line running across the hillside ahead. This is a leat contouring round the hill, and you should aim for that. When you reach it, turn left and follow it round the side of the hill to a sluice gate at a stream. The area to your right as you go round is Trowlesworthy Warren, one of several in this area. Cross the stream and follow the leat on the other side as it goes left round the hill. The area up to your right, above the leat, is Willings Walls Warren, the second warren on your route.

About 750m after crossing the stream, as the leat turns the corner, it cuts through a large Bronze Age settlement. Most of it is to the right of the leat, but there are some remains to the left. (For more information on Bronze Age settlements, see Walk 2.) In the middle of the settlement are the remains of a much later structure, a medieval longhouse.

Follow the leat through the remains and just beyond them branch off half left, away from the leat and towards the wall you can see on the other side of the shallow valley. Cross a stream and make your way up to the left-hand corner of the wall. As you go, you will see the spoil tips thrown up by the ancient miners panning for tin in the stream (for more on tin mining, see Walk 10). You are now in Ditsworthy Warren. Go round the corner and up towards a ruined house, then left past the house to the enclosure just beyond it. Built into the walls of the

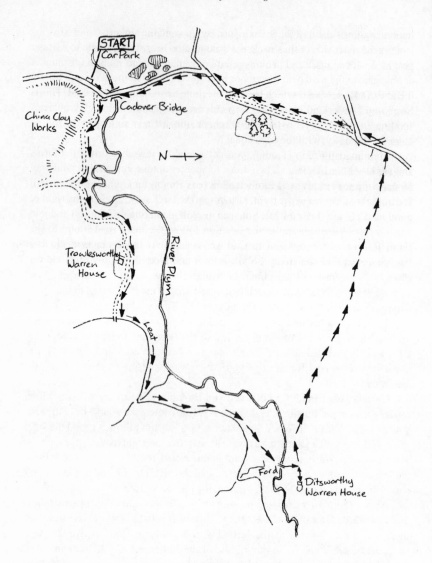

enclosure you can see the stone kennels in which the warrener's dogs were kept.

From the enclosure, turn back the way you came and go round the house. You will find two tracks leading away to the west; the higher one soon curves round to the right, while the lower one goes straight on. Take this one, and as you go look up to the right, where you will see a number of earth mounds; these are the buries which were constructed to encourage the rabbits to burrow and breed. Follow the track down to a gully - this is called a girt, and it was created by miners digging for tin in the hillside leading up from the stream.

On the other side of the girt, leave the track and bear slightly right to a finger post at the fence up ahead. This is a public bridlepath sign pointing through a double gate to the road near Ringmoor Cottage. Go through the gates and follow the line of wooden posts which indicate the route across this private land. This is lovely open moorland with good views all around, just the china clay quarries spoiling the outlook over to the left. There is hardly a tree in sight, just the rolling moors and the sky, with the occasional tor.

After about 1.75km (1 mile), you get a superb view ahead over the farms and woods of west Devon and go down to another double gate. Make your way down to the road below and turn left. You pass Ringmoor Cottage on your left, and as the road curves to the right, turn left up the track which runs to the right of a wall and a fence. After a while you pass a small plantation on your left and join another road. Turn left and at the junction follow the main road round to the right, following the signpost to Cadover Bridge. At the T-junction, go left (signposted to Cadover Bridge, Shaugh Prior and Wotter). Follow this road for about 800m (½ mile) back to Cadover Bridge.

—— 12. Eighteenth-century Water Engineers ——

DEVONPORT LEAT

—————— THE BACKGROUND ——————

Leats are a major feature of Dartmoor. There are probably hundreds of them, and many date back several centuries. Most are fairly short and were only constructed to take water from rivers or rainwater pools to farms and mines. They were built by the farmers and tinners themselves, without any specialist help, and it is a tribute to their skill that so many of them are still operational, even though they may no longer be used for their original purpose.

In the late eighteenth century, however, an undertaking was proposed which required considerable engineering skills - a leat to improve Devonport's water supply. This area, now part of Plymouth, began to be developed as a naval base in the seventeenth and eighteenth centuries, and as it expanded, so did its need for fresh water. It was not the first such leat to be built on Dartmoor; the Plymouth Leat (or Drake's Leat as it is better known) had been built from the River Meavy to Plymouth in the fifteenth century. But it was certainly the most ambitious. Whereas Drake's Leat was only 27km (17 miles) long and ran over comparatively easy terrain, the proposed Devonport Leat was to be 43km (27 miles) long and its course was to extend over some fairly inhospitable moorland. Construction eventually began in 1793, and the leat came into operation in 1801.

The water was taken from the Cowsic and West Dart Rivers and the Blackabrook, with another small intake at the confluence of Hart Tor Brook and the River Meavy, and at one time carried 4.5 million litres (2 million gallons) of water to Devonport every day. Aqueducts were constructed to take it over rivers, such as the one across the Meavy above Burrator Reservoir, and a tunnel took it under a hill near Nun's Cross.

The leat is still operational throughout most of its length, although it now eventually feeds into Burrator Reservoir rather than running all the way to Devonport.

THE WALK

Start and finish: Burrator Reservoir. Grid reference 550680

Parking: There is parking alongside the road near the dam wall. It becomes rather crowded during the summer, however, so you may need to use the parking area on the northern side of the approach road to the west of the reservoir.

Length: 10.5km (6¹/₂ miles)

Approximate time: 3 hours

Degree of difficulty: B

Route summary: From the banks of the reservoir to the moor, this route is full of variety. It takes you through woodland and up to the Devonport Leat as it snakes across the open expanses of Raddick Hill, then back along the leat to the plantation to the north of Burrator. Although it is quite a long walk it is not difficult; the route is clear, the going is easy and there is only one climb.

Starting from the western end of the dam wall, follow the road across the wall and round to the left as it curves round the bottom of the reservoir. As the road goes round to the right, cross a stile on the left and go down to the path alongside the water. The path follows the line of the road, but it makes for rather more pleasant walking. It joins a track, which crosses the second dam wall and curves round to the left, following the reservoir shore.

The track ends at a gate and stile. Go to the left of the stile along a path which runs between the road and the reservoir. After about 400m, you pass a promontory jutting out into the reservoir on your left. Keep to the path that runs alongside the road to cut off the promontory and you will soon see the reservoir on your left again. This whole area is covered in a mixture of conifer and broad-leaved woodland, making it a lovely amble, and although the path is close to the road, you hardly notice it.

The path runs between two walls for a short distance and then you come to a stretch where it becomes rather more difficult to negotiate; you will find yourself having to clamber up a bank and duck below low branches. It is still just passable, but you may prefer to leave the path via one of the stiles on your right and follow the road for a short stretch, rejoining the path about 50-100m further on when the going becomes easier.

About 2km (1¹/₄ miles) after leaving the second dam wall, you come to a track leading down from a gate on your right. Turn right and cross the stile alongside the gate onto the road. Turn left and follow the road round the top of the reservoir to the left. It crosses a bridge and just as it goes to the left across another bridge, turn off right up a track. At the junction go straight on (signposted

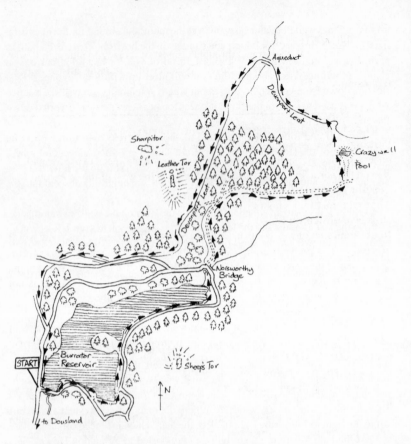

to the county road and Raddick Lane).

The track climbs quite steeply as it curves to the left, then it curves to the right and levels off slightly. Near the top you join another track and finally come out at a gate leading onto the open moor. Keep to the track on the other side and follow it round to the left. As you do so, you will see a cross on the horizon ahead of you. This is one of the crosses marking the Monks' Path, one of the ancient routes across Dartmoor, which was used by monks travelling between Buckfast and Tavistock abbeys (see Walk 8).

As the track crosses a stream running down a gully on your left, turn left to follow the line of the gully. This is called a girt, and it was formed by the digging of medieval tinners as they followed a lode of ore up the hillside (for more on tin mining, see Walk 10). At the top is Crazywell Pool, an old mine working now filled with water. There are several legends associated with it, including one to the effect that at dusk and dawn a voice can be heard coming from it, calling the name of the next person to die in the parish.

Pass Crazywell Pool and carry on over the moorland aiming for the television mast on North Hessary Tor which you can see on the horizon. There is no path as such, but as long as you keep the mast ahead of you, or head due north, you cannot go wrong. After about 250m you will meet up with the Devonport Leat flowing down from your right. Just about where you join it, you will see a sluice which was used to control the flow; if it was too heavy, water was diverted down the gully on the left.

Turn left and follow the leat round the hill, and cross over to the opposite bank at one of the stone bridges. There are some very good views along here across the moors, with the forest around Burrator Reservoir on the left. You pass another sluice, and just beyond it the leat turns left and begins its descent into the valley of the River Meavy down a long cascade.

Follow it down to an aqueduct and cross the river on the walkway alongside. Keep to the leat as it turns to the left on the other side. Look to your left as you go along, and you will see the spoil tips of the original tinners, who panned for ore in the river, on the other side.

The leat eventually goes under a wall to enter Stanlake Plantation. Go down to a stile a few yards on the left to cross the wall yourself and rejoin the leat on the other side. Follow it through the plantation, going straight on at the path junction (signposted to Yennadon Down). Soon you will see Leather Tor looming up to your right beyond the trees.

About 1.25km (³/₄ mile) after entering the plantation, you leave it again via a stile, still following the leat. After another 250m or so you cross another stile back into the plantation and soon after that yet another stile takes you out again and onto a road which crosses the leat. Follow the road, with the whole sweep of Burrator Reservoir now on your left. Where the road crosses the leat again, turn off to the right to follow the right bank of the leat, which is fenced off along here.

At the path junction, go straight on (signposted to Yennadon Down). This takes you along a track through the trees, about 10m from the leat. You soon come alongside it again and turn left to cross a stile and go down some steps to a road. Cross over and go through the gap in the wall on the other side. Turn right (still signposted to Yennadon Down, and still alongside the leat).

Although this is another conifer plantation, the trees are well spaced out, providing enough light for grass to grow and making this a lovely area to walk through. You eventually come out at another road. This is where you leave the leat, which ends soon afterwards, the water passing into a pipeline to the treatment works.

Turn left and follow the road down the hill. At the T-junction turn right to return to the bottom of the reservoir. As you go, you will pass a waterfall on your right. This is caused by surplus water from the leat being diverted straight into the reservoir.

13. Quarrymen to the Nation

HAYTOR QUARRY

THE BACKGROUND

People have been using Dartmoor stone for domestic purposes (huts, houses, walls, gateposts etc) for centuries, but until relatively recently they took only the surface stone. There were two reasons for this: first, with so much available on the surface there was no need to quarry; and secondly, although the people of the moor had the right to collect the surface stone, they had no automatic quarrying rights. It was therefore only towards the end of the eighteenth century that large-scale, commercial quarrying began, with the opening of quarries near Princetown.

The quarry at Haytor, which was owned by the Templer family of Stover, began operations in 1819, although some surface stone had already been taken from there to build Stover House in the late eighteenth century. The company's financial position was shaky, however, and production was sporadic. No granite was produced in the 1840s, and although the quarry reopened in 1850, operations more or less ceased in 1865, except for occasional special orders. The decline was mainly caused by competition from elsewhere, including other Dartmoor quarries; Haytor granite was of a lower quality than that from the Princetown quarries and it was more expensive to transport.

Indeed, granite's popularity generally as a building material at that time is somewhat surprising. Admittedly it is strong and weathers well, but it is difficult to work, and the quarries were more remote than sources of other stone elsewhere in the country. Whatever the reason, however, there is no doubt that it was much sought after. During its short life, the Haytor quarry supplied stone for a number of public buildings, including London Bridge, the British Museum, the National Gallery and Covent Garden.

The stone was extracted from the quarry with gunpowder and picks and then split and cut as required. The traditional method of breaking up larger rocks was by wedge and groove. Slots were cut along the desired line of fracture, and wedges were driven into them. These wedges were probably left in the grooves overnight so that they expanded as the temperature dropped, causing the stone to split. After about 1800, however, the feather-and-tare method came into use, and it was this technique that was used at Haytor. A series of holes were made with a heavy metal chisel called a jumper, then a tapered metal spike (the tare) was hammered in between two metal packing pieces (the feathers). This exerted pressure in the right direction. The remains of the holes can still be seen on several of the reject stones which were left lying around the quarry.

A unique tramway was built to transport the blocks away for shipment. With no foundries in the area, iron rails were not readily available, so granite blocks or setts were used to form the track. There was even an ingenious system of metal 'points' at the junctions. The stone was loaded onto wagons drawn by horses and taken the 13.5km (8¹/₂ miles) down to Teigngrace, a total descent of some 400m (1300ft). There it was transferred to barges on the Stover Canal, which had been built at the end of the eighteenth century primarily to carry ball clay from the Bovey valley. From Teigngrace it was carried down the canal and the River Teign to Teignmouth, where it was shipped to its final destination. The remains of the tramway are still clearly visible in several places around the quarry.

Haytor was one of the first quarries to close, but others followed as the whole Dartmoor granite industry fell into decline. The last quarry to remain in operation, Merrivale, closed in 1997.

THE WALK

Start and finish: Haytor. Grid reference 765771
Parking: In the main car park
Length: 4.25km (2¹/₂ miles)
Approximate time: 1¹/₂ hours
Degree of dificulty: A
Route summary: Haytor Down is open moorland on which you are free to wander at will, so there is no need to stick rigidly to the route I describe. This route does, however, take in most of the points of interest in the Haytor Quarries complex, including the main quarry itself, the granite tramway and the remains of some old workers' cottages. The scenery is superb, and the going is very easy - there is some climbing to get the very best views, but they can easily be avoided if you prefer.

Cross the road and make your way across the moor towards the left of the spoil heaps you can see some distance ahead. There is a fairly clear grassy track leading

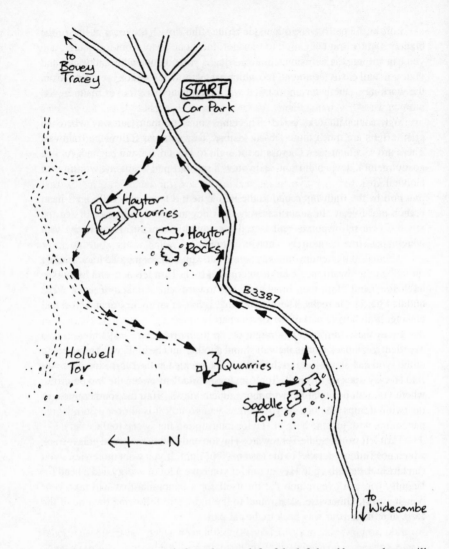

up to them. As you approach them, keep to left of the left-hand heap and you will come to a gate in a fence. Just before you go through the gate, look at the pile of reject rocks on your left. You will see that some of them have grooves down the side; this is where the tare and feathers were inserted to split the stone.

Go through the gate and turn left along the top of the workings ahead of you. This path leads you to the main quarry, which is now filled with water. Follow it round to the left of the quarry, and as you go you will see the remains of some of the equipment used when it was still working, including a winch. The path then leaves the quarry via a stile on the opposite side from where you came in.

Follow the path on the other side of the stile. This is the route of one of the branches of the tramway used to transport the stone away from the quarry, and you can still see the occasional granite sett. As you go, look at the stones around you; you will easily be able to see which are natural and which are rejects from the workings - the latter are marked with the distinctive grooves made by the jumper.

Where the path forks, go left. This takes you to the main tramway, where the granite setts are much more clearly visible. Turn left and follow the tramway. There are excellent views across to the right to Hound Tor and beyond. As you go along, look down half right, and you will see the spoil heaps and workings of Holwell Tor.

Follow the tramway round to the left. Where it forks, ignore the left-hand branch and follow the main tramway. Just beyond the fork, you will see the remains of a set of points, and then the tramway peters out. Keep to the path which goes straight on in the same direction.

About 200m after the tramway peters out, you will see a broad track leading off to the left, towards some large outcrops of rock. Turn left here and follow the track for about 50m, then branch off left towards the remains of some walls huddled below the rocks. These are all that is left of an enclosure and workers' cottages which were part of the Harrowbarrow quarry.

From these remains, go straight on up to the ridge of rocks above for an excellent view back across the valley and another up ahead. If you prefer not to climb, you can skirt round to the right of the rocks. On the other side, you will find an easy track up to Saddle Tor. Aim for the saddle between the two outcrops, where you will be rewarded with more superb views; from the southernmost of the two outcrops (the one on your left as you go up), it is almost a 360-degree panorama, with just the bulk of Haytor interrupting the sweep to the east.

Turn left from Saddle Tor towards Haytor, and follow the broad grassy track which goes almost parallel to the road on your right. If you want more views you can tackle the climb up to Haytor (and if you have a lot of energy and a head for heights, you can even climb the tor itself for a panorama that will take your breath away). Otherwise, skirt round to the right, still following the line of the road, and make your way back to the car park.

14. Sir Thomas Tyrwhitt's Railway

BRIDGE ON THE PLYMOUTH AND DARTMOOR RAILWAY

THE BACKGROUND

Born in Essex, Sir Thomas Tyrwhitt settled at Tor Royal, near what is now Princetown. He was a personal friend and Private Secretary of the Prince Regent, and became Lord Warden of the Stannaries. He had a dream of opening up and 'civilising' central Dartmoor by encouraging cultivation and exploiting the large granite reserves.

The first stage in his plan was to found Princetown (named after his friend the Prince Regent) as the centre of this new community towards the end of the eighteenth century. Quarrying began in the area at about the same time. He then persuaded the government to build a prison there for French prisoners from the Napoleonic Wars. Construction was begun in 1806 and the first prisoners arrived in 1809. In 1813 they were joined by Americans. The establishment was closed in 1816, but reopened as a civilian prison in 1850, and still continues to dominate the village.

But the cornerstone of his project was a railway linking Princetown with Plymouth. The plan was that it would bring in lime and sea sand to make the land more fertile so that crops could be grown, as well as timber and household items for the new settlers who were expected, and that it would carry granite, peat and produce down to the city. Tyrwhitt made a proposal to this effect to the Plymouth Chamber of Commerce and the route was surveyed. The Act enabling the Plymouth and Dartmoor Railway to be established was passed in 1819 and the line was opened in 1823 - the first iron railway in Devon.

The project was dogged by financial problems from the start, however. Even during its construction there were a number of crises as the costs overran the capital that had been raised. The problems continued after its opening. It was found that the moor could not be made cultivable simply by the application of lime and sea sand - good news for the Dartmoor landscape but disastrous for the railway, as it now had to rely on the export of granite for most of its income. This income was not enough to cover the company's expenses, and it was not until 1870 that the first dividend was declared - and that was a mere 5s (25p) per 100 share.

The line was originally more like a tramway than a railway. It had a 4¹/₂ft gauge track, with wagons drawn by horses. By the 1870s, however, it was becoming clear that a proper railway was required if the needs of Princetown's expanding population were to be met, and in 1881 the line was taken over by the Princetown Railway Company, a subsidiary of the Great Western Railway. A new track was laid and the line reopened in 1883 as a steam railway carrying both passengers and freight. It was finally closed in 1956.

THE WALK
Start and finish: Princetown. Grid reference 589735
Parking: In the public car park behind the High Moorland Visitor Centre
Length: 5.5km (3¹/₂ miles)
Degree of difficulty: A
Links with: Walk 1
Route summary: A short and easy amble along part of the route of the Plymouth and Dartmoor Railway to Foggintor, one of the granite quarries that provided much of its income. From Foggintor, there is a short stretch of open moor up to North Hessary Tor, with some superb views to the south and east, before you join a path back to Princetown. Alternatively, you can imagine that you are a traveller of old and follow part of the ancient Tavistock to Ashburton packhorse route back; if you do so, however, you will miss some of the views.

Leave the car park by the vehicle entrance and turn left at the road. Just beyond the fire station, bear left along a path between fences, following the sign pointing to the disused railway. The path leads to a gate and continues on the other side, with a fence on the right and a ditch on the left. Follow the path alongside a conifer plantation to join a track, which is the old railway line. As you go, you will see a broad sweep of moorland half left, with a number of tors and the forest above Burrator Reservoir.

You cross a bridge and the track curves to the right. You now get a very good view ahead, across farmland to the northern moors. The track continues to wind along the contour of the hill, crossing another bridge, and then, about 2km (1¹/₄ miles) from the start, it takes a long curve to the right. As it straightens out, it crosses another track. Turn right here to reach Foggintor Quarries.

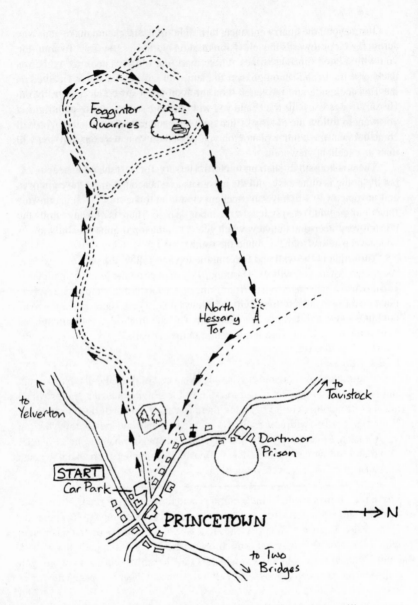

Follow this new track between some large spoil tips and you will soon see the remains of the quarry buildings. The track goes to the right of the buildings and you will see the entrance to the quarry itself on your right. (For more information on quarrying, see Walk 13.) The quarry makes an excellent place to stop for a picnic.

Just beyond the quarry entrance, turn right off the track and make your way across the moor towards the television mast on North Hessary Tor. To your left, you will see two upright stones. These mark the old Tavistock to Ashburton packhorse track, and if you go over to them, you will see the letter T carved on the Tavistock side and the letter A on the Ashburton side. The route to North Hessary Tor crosses this track, and you will see more stones over to your right; if you want to follow the old track, turn right here and follow the stones. You will come out near the conifer plantation you passed on your way out, but you will miss an excellent viewpoint.

There is no path as such up to North Hessary Tor, just the odd sheep track, but the going is quite easy, and the mast acts as a beacon. Aim to the right of it, and as you go you will have an excellent view over to the right. You get the true flavour of the wide open spaces of the moor up here. There is a steady climb, but it is not very steep and the view when you get to the top is quite breathtaking - a wide sweep across to the east and the south.

Turn right at the wall and fence at the top and follow the path alongside it. As you go down, you will see Dartmoor Prison over on the left. The path takes you down to a gate on the outskirts of Princetown. Go through it to a road. Where the road turns to the left, turn right to follow a path. There is no sign at the road, but there is one a few yards along the path. Cross a footbridge and join another road at the fire station. Turn left to return to the car park.

15. Nineteenth-century Miners

WHEAL BETSY

THE BACKGROUND

Although tin was the main mineral found in the granite area of Dartmoor, there were a number of others to be found in the metamorphic aureole - the area on the edge of the moor where the sedimentary rock has not been eroded - including copper, lead, zinc, silver, arsenic and iron.

Where the lodes of ore were above the valley floor, horizontal tunnels called adits were dug into the hillsides, and water could drain out naturally. But the major exploitation of these deposits really only began in the nineteenth century as new technology made the sinking of shafts and the pumping out of water possible (see Walk 10). It is not known when Wheal Betsy first became operational, for example, but it was closed in the eighteenth century and only reopened, using the new technology, in 1806. And although copper and lead production is known to have taken place at Wheal Friendship as early as 1714, it too ceased production for a time, only recommencing operations in 1796. Water power was initially used to operate the new machinery, and it was some time before it was replaced by steam - in the case of Wheal Betsy not until 1868.

Copper was probably the most important of the 'new' minerals on Dartmoor. In the early nineteenth century, over 40 per cent of the world's copper came from Devon and Cornwall, and there were about 40 mines in the Dartmoor area. But in many cases, more than one mineral was extracted from each mine: copper, lead and later arsenic at Wheal Friendship, for example, copper, lead, silver and arsenic at Wheal Betsy and tin followed by arsenic at Wheal Jewell.

The 'lifespans' of these mines obviously varied considerably, depending on the extent of the deposits and the availability of alternative sources of income when the original deposits ceased to be viable. Wheal Jewell, for example, did not open until 1865, and was only operational for a few decades. Wheal Betsy lasted somewhat longer; having reopened in 1806, it did not close until 1877. And although copper mining at Wheal Friendship ceased in 1870, arsenic production lasted into this century.

THE WALK

Start and finish: Zoar, about 700m (¹/₂ mile) north-east of Horndon, near Mary Tavy. Grid reference 523806
Parking: You can pull in up a track on the northern side of the road, just opposite some cottages.
Length: 8.5km (5¹/₄ miles)
Approximate time: 2¹/₂ hours
Degree of difficulty: B
Route summary: The remains of Wheal Jewell, Wheal Betsy and Wheal Friendship are all within relatively easy reach of each other, and this route takes them all in. It enables you to experience both moorland and riverside walking without too much effort - there is little climbing, and the route is clear throughout.

Follow the track north, away from the road. When the wall on your right turns to the right, follow it round. When it goes right again, follow it again. You get a good view of the open moor ahead of you.

As you go down, you will see some of the old shafts of Wheal Jewell, fenced off to avoid people and sheep falling into them, on your right. Follow the track that leads away from the wall to another shaft. Just beyond this shaft you will find a broken wall with a stream just in front of it. Cross the stream and turn left to follow it up to a large bank which forms the side of Wheal Jewell Reservoir.

There is a path leading up the bank, from which you can see this small and rather unattractive reservoir. It was not part of the original Wheal Jewell complex - it was not opened until 1936 - but the leat which feeds it was. There is a choice of two concrete bridges crossing the leat, depending on where you came up the bank. Take either, but once across, join the track leading off half left from the right-hand bridge.

Follow the track as it curves to the left, passing a post with the top painted green. Ignore the track which goes off to the right, but go half right immediately after passing it, to follow a line of green-painted posts which mark the path across Kingsett Down.

As you go, you will see the chimney of the Wheal Betsy engine house half right, and as you come across the brow of the down the whole engine house will come into view. It is marvellously still up here, with good views. Follow the posts round to the left until you meet a wide, well-worn track crossing your path.

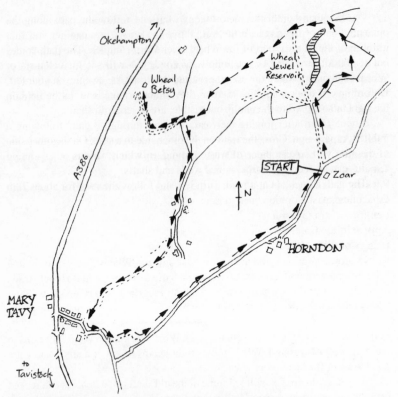

Turn right and follow the track to a gate with a bridlepath sign.

Go through the gate and down the track across the field. On the other side, the track goes right and down the hillside to another gate. Go through it to a road, cross the river and as the road bends to the left, go right up a track to reach Wheal Betsy.

When you have explored Wheal Betsy, retrace your steps down the track, across the river and through the gate on the other side. Follow the track through the field to the gate you came through originally. Once through this gate and back on Kingsett Down, turn right and follow a track alongside the wall to another gate. Go through and follow the track on the other side. This leads down to a farm, where it joins a surfaced lane. Carry straight on. After about 300m you will find a track on the left. Immediately opposite it is a public footpath sign. Turn right, following the direction of the sign, over a stone stile.

Go straight across the field on the other side to another stile, then another field to a third stile. Keep to the path which follows the line of the stream on your right, crossing more stiles as you go. The path finally goes to the right to cross the stream via a footbridge. It can be rather muddy along here, so you should proceed with care.

On the other side of the footbridge, go left and follow the path along the opposite bank of the river. To the left, above the gorse, you can get you first glimpse of the ruins of part of the Wheal Friendship complex. The path comes out at a road; turn left. As you follow the road, you will see the calciners of Wheal Friendship, where the ore was roasted to extract the arsenic, on your left. Unfortunately, one cannot visit them as they are on private land. In the field on the right, also closed to the public but visible, are several old shafts.

About 150m after joining the road, turn left through a gate, following a public footpath sign. Cross the field on the other side to a stile. On the other side of the stile you cross a piece of waste ground, in which various other mining remains can be seen: spoil tips, ruined walls and shafts.

The path comes out at a road. Turn left and follow the road for about 2km (1$\frac{1}{4}$ miles), past Horndon back to Zoar.

16. Victorian Powder Manufacturers

POWDER MILLS

THE BACKGROUND

Until the invention of dynamite in 1867, rock or black powder - a mixture of charcoal, saltpetre and sulphur - was used for blasting in the quarries and mines of Britain. Indeed, it continued to be used in the quarries for some time after dynamite appeared on the scene, as the latter tended to shatter the rock, whereas rock powder broke it off more cleanly.

The Powder Mills, near Postbridge, started manufacturing rock powder in 1844, and production continued until the late 1890s. The process involved boiling and crystallising the saltpetre before grinding it between stones driven by a water wheel. It was then mixed with the other ingredients and churned, then pressed into cakes, which were broken, glazed and dried. The quality of the powder was tested in a mortar which can still be seen between the road and the buildings which now house the Powder Mills Craft Centre (once the mill's offices and living quarters). An iron ball weighing 68lb was fired from the mortar, and the powder classified according to the distance it travelled.

This isolated site was chosen deliberately, in order to minimise the risk of loss of life in the event of an accident. Indeed, because of the volatility of the powder, safety was a major feature of the design and working of the mill. For example, the chimneys were very tall, so that the fumes were dispersed away from the buildings and the risk of sparks setting light to the powder was minimised. And although the walls of the buildings were very solidly built, the roofs were flimsy constructions of wood and tar, so that if there was an explosion, the force of the blast would be dissipated through the roof, which would blow off fairly easily. As you will see, the buildings were also located at some distance from each other, so that a fire in one would not spread to the others.

Another safety precaution was that all workers were required to take off their boots when they entered any of the buildings, in case the nails on the soles struck sparks from the stone floors. In fact, so aware was the workforce of the dangers of the place that one man is said to have eaten both his lunch and his dinner together each day, in case he was killed by an explosion in the afternoon, before he had had time to eat his evening meal!

THE WALK

Start and finish: Higher Cherrybrook Bridge, near Postbridge. Grid reference 635770

Parking: The car park a few yards north-east of the bridge

Length: 8.5km (5¼ miles)

Approximate time: 2½ hours

Degree of difficulty: B

Links with: Walks 7 and 9

Route summary: You follow part of the Lich Path or Lichway, one of the ancient transmoor routes, to the remains of the Powder Mills, then climb up to Littaford Tors, Longaford Tor and Higher White Tor for superb views of the surrounding moor. There is more moorland walking to Postbridge, from where you follow a forest track to rejoin the Lich Path back to the car park. There are one or two boggy stretches to negotiate, but apart from that it is a relatively easy walk.

Cross the road to a gate, following the Lichway sign. You are now on the Lich Path or Lichway, the ancient route taken by residents of this side of the moor as they crossed to Lydford to bury their dead (see Walk 8). You will see the chimney of the Powder Mills slightly to your left as you go through the gate, and that is where you are heading. It is unlikely that you will be able to cut straight across to it, however, as there is a large stretch of marsh ahead. You will therefore have to go up to your right to skirt round it - how far you will have to go depends on how much rain there has been and how wet it is underfoot. Once across you should aim for the gate you can see in the wall just in front of the chimney.

Go through the gate and follow the blue-arrowed posts among the buildings. Do not be tempted to leave the path and explore the buildings themselves; they could be dangerous. Moreover, this is private land, and the only public access is along the marked path. You cross a stream and go through a gate on the other side, marked 'Bridlepath'. Follow the path up to the left to another gate and go slightly right to yet another gate leading onto the moor.

Carry straight on, aiming slightly to the right of the piles of rocks you can see up ahead, which are Littaford Tors. The path is quite clear, but it does not matter if you deviate slightly, as there is open access on this part of the moor and you

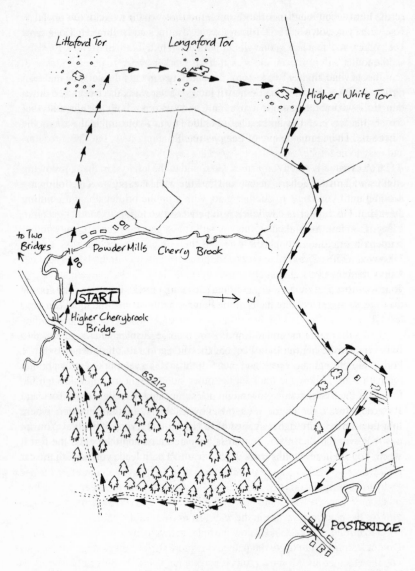

can always correct yourself when you get to the wall near the top of the ridge if necessary. You pass a very rocky stretch and then you will see a ladder stile on the wall ahead. Cross the stile and continue on the path up the hill.

When you reach the top, you will see the rocks of Littaford Tors on your left and the dome of Longaford Tor on your right, with a track running between them. From up here there is a magnificent 180-degree panorama behind you, across farms, woods and moorland, and a good view of the range of tors ahead of you, with Princetown half left. Turn right onto the track and follow it to Longaford Tor. When you reach it, you will see Higher White Tor half right. Cross the saddle to it.

Just beyond Higher White Tor is a wall. Cross it via a ladder stile and turn right to follow it down the hill. Where it joins another wall, turn left and go down into Hollowcombe Bottom to cross the Cherry Brook. Make for the stile that crosses the fence and wall ahead of you and keep to your original wall on the other side. There are a couple of boggy stretches along here, but they are short and easy to negotiate.

You eventually reach some trees. Go round to the left to skirt them, following another wall round. You pass a gate and then the wall bears right. Keep following it round until you come to another gate, with a public bridlepath sign pointing through it. Go through and follow a path between two fences to another gate into a lane. Turn left. After about 250m you will find a gate on your left, and another bridlepath sign. Go through the gate and then diagonally right across a field, following a line of short blue posts. Go through a gateway in the far corner, and follow the blue posts diagonally across the next field. Cross a stream and make your way to a gate in the corner of the field onto a track. Turn right and follow the track to a road, passing the Postbridge information centre and toilets on your left.

Cross the main road and follow the side road on the other side, signposted to Bellever, across a cattle grid. Just beyond the cattle grid, turn off right into Bellever Forest. Go through a car park and then left through a gate marked with a public footpath sign. Follow the track on the other side straight up a hill through the forest. At the first junction, go straight on (signposted to Bellever and Tor), and at the next fork right (signposted to Bellever Tor). At the third junction, where four tracks meet, turn right (signposted to Higher Cherrybrook Bridge). You are now back on the Lich Path. You cross a cleared area and then enter the forest again. You finally leave the trees via a stile and a path leads you back to the car park.

17. Turn-of-the-century Peat Cutters

BLEAK HOUSE

THE BACKGROUND

Peat is formed by the decomposition of vegetable matter in wet conditions - in fact just the conditions found on the high northern moor. Its main use in the past was as a domestic fuel, but it also had some industrial applications; it was used on Dartmoor by the early tinners and also in the later shaft mines.

As an industry, peat extraction reached its peak in the mid-nineteenth century. Production at the Rattlebrook Peatworks probably began in the 1850s, although the earliest records that remain only date back to 1868. The peat was cut with a triangular shovel called a budding iron. The roots were then trimmed with a knife and slabs dug out with a tool called a turf iron. The top layers were taken for domestic use and the deeper levels for industrial peat, and it was reckoned that a good cutter could cut 1,440 slabs in half a day.

A tramway, with trucks pulled by men, took the peat from the peat ties where it was cut to the works. A railway was opened in 1879 to take it from there down to the London & SW Railway at Bridestowe. This line was used until the 1930s, when it was replaced by lorries.

In addition to its use as a fuel, peat could also be used to produce petrol, tar oil and naphtha. The latter was made into candles which gave a very bright light and were used a great deal in mining.

The enterprise was beset by difficulties from quite early in its life; indeed, work stopped completely in 1880 because of the high cost of the railway. Another problem was that it was difficult to dry the peat. The moist moorland air prevented it being dried in the open, and although both pressing and oven drying were tried, neither was very successful.

Various plans were devised to revitalise the works in the early part of this century, but few came to fruition. A German scientist claimed to have developed a process for distilling alcohol from peat, but died before he could put it into practice. There was also a scheme for producing petrol, and a plan for a health hydro offering peat baths, but these were both scuppered by the outbreak of the Second World War. Despite these setbacks, however, production continued until the 1950s, when the peat was sold for horticultural use.

THE WALK

Start and finish: The parking area just behind the Dartmoor Inn on the A386 outside Lydford. Grid reference 525853
Parking: In the parking area
Length: 10km (6¹/₄ miles)
Approximate time: 3 hours
Degree of difficulty: B
Links with: Walk 4
Route summary: The north-western corner of Dartmoor is an awesome place; there are no roads (and few tracks), no settlements, just mile upon mile of barren moorland, steep-sided valleys and high tors. This route gives you a taste of its wildness without taking you too far from civilisation. You go up to the Rattlebrook Peatworks and then back along the track of the tramway that took the peat down to join the railway line at Bridestowe. There are easy markers to help you find your way, but you do have to negotiate one steep hill and some marshy stretches.

Head off towards the open moor from the parking area, going slightly left to join a track running alongside a wall. Follow the track to cross the River Lyd, either via the stepping stones or via the footbridge a few yards upstream. Continue to follow the track as it winds to the left and then to the right, becoming less clear as it does so.

When the track starts to go left again, branch off to the right to climb up to the saddle between Arms Tor on the left and Brat Tor on the right. It is a long, stiff climb and near the top you have to pick your way between some rather marshy areas, but when you reach the top of the saddle you are rewarded with a magnificent view back across the lush, rolling farmland of West Devon and East Cornwall.

From the top of the saddle, keep going straight on, along the lower slopes of the hill on your left. You will probably meet up with a track; if so, you can follow it, although it can be rather wet as it usually has a rivulet running down it. If you do not meet the track, do not worry; as long as you keep the hill on your left, you are going the right way. As you follow the line of the track, you will see a deep gully running down on your right. This is called a girt, and was formed by miners of old digging for tin (for more on tin mining, see Walk 10).

Soon you will see the rocks of Great Links Tor on your left, and then you

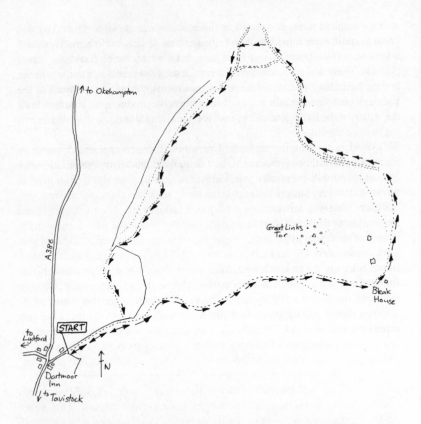

pass another girt stretching up towards it. Just by the girt you will see a stone standing up alongside the track. This is an old boundary stone marking the point where the commons of Bridestowe and Sourton and the Forest of Dartmoor met. You will notice the letter 'L' engraved on the side nearest the track (for Lydford, the parish in which the Forest of Dartmoor lay) and 'BS' on the other side (for Bridestowe and Sourton).

A little way beyond the girt there is a fork in the track. Follow the left-hand route, and soon a whole sweep of open moorland appears ahead of you, with not a tree, a road or a building in sight. On your left you will see the rocks of Lower Dunna Goat and beyond them those of Higher Dunna Goat. The track more or less peters out at a girt running off to the right. Bear left and make your way round Lower Dunna Goat. Soon a ruined house comes into view ahead of you across the Rattle Brook. This is now aptly called Bleak House, but its original name was Dunnagoat Cottage and it was built for the manager of the peatworks.

There is a good place to cross the brook about 100m below Bleak House. Walk up to Bleak House and then continue to follow the brook upstream. You may need to climb away from it in places to avoid marshy stretches. Soon you will see some of the peat ties, where the peat was cut, on your right. You will come to some more ruined buildings, the remains of the works themselves, with a very clear track leading away from them to your left. Turn left onto it.

This is the line of the old tramway which took the peat down to the railway. It goes first along an embankment and then through a cutting. It winds to the right and you get an excellent view, and then another opens up to your left down the valley of the Lyd. Continue to follow the track as it bends to the left to cross the head of the valley.

Shortly after crossing the infant Lyd, you will see another track coming up from your left, following the line of the valley. This is also part of the Rattlebrook tramway, and will eventually join your track over to your right. You need to follow it down the valley, so to avoid having to walk two sides of a triangle, you can make your way across the grass to join it and turn left. The track goes round to the right of a hill and then bears right slightly, towards a wall. It ends just to the left of the corner of the wall. Turn right and go through the gate ahead of you. Turn immediately left and left again to go through another gate and then turn right, following the footpath sign. After about 100m you come to another sign; follow the path that goes half left away from the wall. The route is quite clear, as it follows the line of a slight dip in the ground, but where the dip curves to the left, you should go straight on to a gate in the wall ahead. Cross the stone stile across the wall alongside it and turn right along the track on the other side to return to the parking area.

── 18. Twentieth-century China Clay Diggers ──

RED LAKE

────────────────── **THE BACKGROUND** ──────────────────

During the cooling of the granite over 250 million years ago, some of the felspar (one of the three constituents of granite) softened and formed china clay or kaolin. The main deposits of this china clay are found in the south-west of Dartmoor, and it is used in the production of a wide range of products, including ceramics, paper, pharmaceuticals, plastics and paint.

The only china clay quarry still operating on Dartmoor is the extensive workings at Lee Moor, which opened in 1830. There are, however, three abandoned pits in and around the Erme valley: Left Lake, Petre's Pit and Red Lake. Of these, Red Lake was the most important, and also the most recent. Petre's Pit and Left Lake only produced clay for about eight years each in the latter half of the last century (although Left Lake was reopened for a few years in the 1920s as part of the Red Lake complex), whereas Red Lake operated from 1913 to 1932.

The extraction process involved the removal of the topsoil before the clay was washed out with high-pressure hoses called monitors. It went through various procedures to remove the sand and mica and passed into settling pits, where excess water was drained off and evaporated. It was then transferred, suspended in water, by pipeline to the Cantrell works, near Bittaford, for drying. The clay from the smaller workings at Petre's Pit travelled, also in suspension, by leat to works at Shipley Bridge, where the remains of the old settling tanks and drying sheds can still be seen.

At Cantrell and Shipley Bridge, more of the water was drained off in settling tanks, and the clay was transferred to drying sheds where it was spread out on the floor and dried still further by heat.

A railway was built from Bittaford to Red Lake between 1910 and 1912 to carry men and equipment to and from the workings (although many of the men stayed in a hostel at Red Lake during the week), and to take waste sand back to be sold as fertiliser. The workings at Petre's Pit were able to make use of an existing line, the Zeal Tor tramway. Originally built to bring peat from the Red Lake area to naphtha works at Shipley Bridge between 1847 and 1850, it was brought into use again when the china clay workings were opened in 1872, to carry men and equipment up to the pit. But whereas the Red Lake line was a proper railway using steam locomotives, the Zeal Tor tramway was just that - a tramway with trucks drawn by horses. Unusually, the rails were made of wood, and were bolted to individual granite blocks with no sleepers.

The clay at Red Lake was of a very much lower quality than that at Lee Moor, and the China Clay Corporation, which owned the works, consequently suffered more than its rival from the slump in demand during the First World War. The company went into receivership in 1919 and although it was sold in 1920, it never fully recovered and finally ceased production in 1932.

THE WALK

Start and finish: Shipley Bridge, between South Brent and the Avon Dam. Grid reference 681629

Parking: There is a car park at Shipley Bridge.

Length: 16km (10 miles)

Approximate time: 4¹/₂ -5 hours

Degree of difficulty: C

Links with: Walk 8

Route summary: I have classified this walk as C because of its length, but it is not actually very difficult in terms of either navigation or terrain. There are virtually no steep ascents and the route is clear throughout, yet it takes you up onto the wide, lonely moorland, with excellent views from time to time. It follows the track of the Zeal Tor tramway up to the Red Lake works and returns via the Red Lake railway line, passing Petre's Pit on the way up and Left Lake on the way back.

The ruins on the left-hand side of the car park as you enter are those of the drying sheds used for the Petre's Pit clay, with the remains of the settling tanks behind. There is nothing left of the naphtha works, which were demolished to make way for these buildings.

Take the path which goes past the toilets and joins a road alongside the River Avon. This is a lovely stretch, with oaks and rhododendrons on the other side. At the road junction, you will see a stone on your left with some names carved on it. This is the Hunters' Stone, which commemorates well-known members of of the local hunt. At the beginning of the century, there were just four names - Treby, Trelawney and Bulteel on the sides and Carew on the top - but more have been added since then.

Turn left at the junction for a steady but not too steep climb along the hill. At the gate to the water treatment works at the end, turn right and follow a sunken track alongside the wall. When the wall veers off to the left, carry straight on and join the clear track which is slightly to your right. This is the route of the Zeal Tor tramway, and you will occasionally come across some of the stones to which the rails were attached, still with the bolts embedded in them. You continue to climb, but rather more gently now. There is a tremendous sense of peace and tranquillity up here, with just the occasional call of a meadow pipit and the murmuring of the Bala Brook down on your left to break the silence. The farmland of the Dartmoor 'in country' stretches away behind you, with the rolling hills of the moor itself ahead.

As the tramline goes to the right, you see the strange shape of Eastern White Barrow on the horizon ahead. This is an ancient burial chamber, although its shape is a comparatively recent phenomenon. No one knows who built it up into its present formation, or why. As you near the head of the valley, the track turns to the left. It becomes less obviously a tramway as it does so, but there is still a clear path. Soon you will find the brook coming up to about 20m from the path on your left. Towards the top you will see the spoil tips of some old tin workings (for more on tin mining, see Walk 10) and further on, at the very top of the valley, Petre's Pit is visible about 100m away on your left.

The line of the tramway is now visible again as a shallow gully. As you come over the brow of the hill, another superb vista opens up ahead, with the moorland stretching away, and on your left you can see all the way down the valley to Plymouth and the sea. As the tramway contours round to the right the white scars of the modern china clay works at Lee Moor also come into view down the valley on the left, and ahead you will see the cairn on Western White Barrow.

The tramway passes to the left of the cairn. At the crest of the hill, another superb sweep of moorland appears ahead and to left and right. Ahead of you you can see the conical shape of the spoil tip of the Red Lake works. About 500m beyond Western White Barrow you will see the remains of some settling tanks on your left. Pass them, and the track becomes less obvious. There is still a path, however, which you should follow towards the Red Lake spoil tip. When you meet a track crossing your path, turn right. This is the line of the Red Lake railway, and you can follow it all the way to the quarry. The latter is now filled with water and makes a good place to stop for a picnic.

Retrace your steps along the railway track, but where it goes to the right follow it round rather than going straight up past the settling tanks again. The track takes a sharp turn to the left, and as it straightens out again, you will see some mounds on your left; these are the remains of more old tin workings. As you go along here, you get a very good view down the valley to Plymouth again.

Shortly after the track turns to the right again, you will cross a gully. If you look to your left, you will see an arched concrete structure. This is an aqueduct which took the pipeline carrying the china clay suspension across the gully. After a while the track turns sharply to the left again. Just before it does so you will see a stone on either side, about 20-30m from the track. These are part of a long line of stones, prehistoric in origin but used in medieval times as markers delineating the boundaries between the lands of different landowners and parishes.

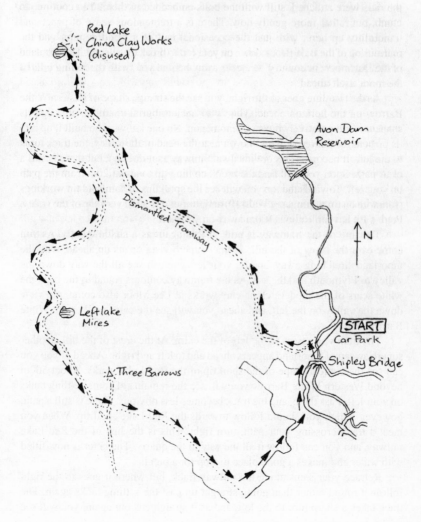

As the track turns to the right again, look to your right and you will see another aqueduct carrying the china clay pipeline across a gully, and soon afterwards you come to the Left Lake workings, with the main pit on your left but some diggings to your right. As the track curves to the left again you get another superb view down to the valley across farmland to the sea.

Just before a right-hand bend you cross the line of boundary stones again, this time clearer than before, and you can see the stones stretching away on your right. About 900m after crossing the line, as the track takes a slight turn to the right, you will see a grassy track coming down from the hillside on the left to join it. This is where you leave the Red Lake railway to cut up left across the moor.

There is no clear path, but ahead of you is a prominent hill topped by some rocks. Aim to the right of this hill and to the left of the small stream which soon comes into view below it. You go down into a dip and contour round the hill a short distance from the stream. As you go round you will see a wall up ahead with a track leading away from you on the other side of the next hill. That is the approximate direction in which you should be aiming. You will find that there is a narrow path you can follow.

Shortly before you reach the wall, go left to cut off an angle and meet the wall at a corner. Follow the wall beyond the corner and when another wall comes in from the left go between the two. When the left-hand wall veers away, keep following the right-hand one to a gate. Go through it and follow a wet, rocky path which takes you steeply down between two walls to another gate onto a road. Turn left and follow the road to the right to cross a stream, then left up a hill to a cattle grid. Beyond the cattle grid, follow the road round to the right to return to the car park.

CASTLE DROGO

———— THE BACKGROUND ————

Country house life in the inter-war years generally revolved around the ancient houses and families of Britain, but there were also the 'nouveaux riches' - mainly industrialists and businessmen - who developed a taste for the ways of the landed gentry.

One such was Julius Drew. His grandfather had been a tea broker and Julius went into the same business. He soon set up on his own, however, opening a shop in Liverpool in 1878. In 1883, he and a partner opened the Home and Colonial Stores in London, and by 1890, there were 107 branches across the country. Although he was only 33, Drew was by then wealthy enough to leave the running of the company to others and cultivate the lifestyle of a country gentleman.

He settled in Sussex initially, but soon began to look west. Family tradition had it that the Drews originated in Devon. A genealogist suggested that they were descended from the Drewe family who lived near Honiton, and Julius therefore added a final 'e' to his name in 1910. The genealogist also showed that one of his direct ancestors might have been a Norman baron called Drogo, whose descendant, Drogo de Teigne, gave his name to Drewsteignton, on the north-eastern fringes of Dartmoor.

It happened that Drewe's cousin was rector of Drewsteignton, and that he owned land adjoining the Teign Gorge in the parish. Drewe was therefore able to acquire it and commissioned the famous architect Sir Edwin Lutyens to design him a castle to stand on a promontory above the gorge, with magnificent views up the valley to the moors. The result is Castle Drogo, which was built between 1911 and 1930. Over the years he bought other parcels of land so that at the time of his death he owned some 1,500 acres.

Lutyens's original design envisaged a house some three times larger than the one you see today, with four wings surrounding a courtyard. For a variety of reasons, that proved impractical, and the size was gradually reduced,with only two wings actually being built. On one thing, however, Drewe insisted that there should be no compromise: the castle was to be built along traditional lines. There were to be no bricks faced with stone, just solid local granite.

Drewe's occupancy of his new home was sadly brief; he died just a few years after moving in. The house (the term 'castle' is perhaps somewhat fanciful) passed to his son Basil and then to his grandson Anthony. It is now in the hands of the National Trust.

The interior is furnished much as it would have been in Julius Drewe's time, and gives an excellent impression of country house life in the 1930s. There were the usual country pursuits of shooting and fishing on the estate, and the equipment used can still be seen in the gun room. Tea (which could last as long as two hours) was taken in the library and billard room, but all other meals were served in the large and formal dining room. The drawing room was used for entertaining, and for taking coffee after dinner; the family's favourite room for more informal gatherings was the library and billard room.

A great many servants were needed to keep the house running smoothly and to serve the family and guests. Although the numbers fluctuated, there were always at least 11 in the house itself: a butler, an under-butler, a cook, a kitchen maid, a scullery maid, two housemaids, two ladies' maids, a nursery maid and a nanny. Outside, there would have been a chauffeur, a groom and seven gardeners.

THE WALK

Start and finish: Drewsteignton. Grid reference 735908
Parking: In the village square, by the church
Length: 8.5km (5¼ miles)
Approximate time: The walk itself will take about 2 -3 hours, but you should allow time to explore Castle Drogo.
Degree of difficulty: B
Route summary: The Teign Gorge is an outstandingly beautiful area, with its steep sides covered in gorse and heather and the river flowing through sun-dappled woodland at the bottom. And the views from the top (especially from Castle Drogo) are magnificent. This route takes you through much of the Drogo Estate - above the gorge to Castle Drogo and then through the woods alongside the river - before returning to Drewsteignton through more woodland. There are some stiff climbs, but the views when you reach the top are worth the effort. *Castle Drogo is a National Trust property. It is only open from the end of March to the end of October (closed on Fridays), from 11.00 a.m. to 5.30 p.m., and there is an*

entrance fee for non-members.

Go left from the village square and at the road junction, turn right (signposted to Whiddon Down, Chagford, Moretonhampstead and Castle Drogo). Just on the edge of the village, turn left down a track (signposted to the Hunter's Path, Fingle Bridge and the road near Castle Drogo). The track leads down to a gate, where it turns sharp right.

At the bottom, you cross a stream and on the other side go right (signposted to the Hunter's Path). The footpath climbs steeply among the trees, and near the top there are some steps to make the going a bit easier. At the top, you cross a stile and follow the fence on your right to cross a field. At the top of the field you cross another stile and continue along the fence on your right. As you go, you get an excellent view across the valley.

Cross another stile at the end of the field and go down a few yards to join the Hunter's Path. Turn right (signposted to the road near Drogo and the Fisherman's Path). The path takes you high above the Teign Gorge and you get a superb view up the valley. As you go round a bend you will see Castle Drogo on a promontory up ahead. Soon you will come to a path leading off to the right (signposted to Castle Drogo and garden). Turn off here and follow the path up to the castle drive, where you turn left to visit the castle and its beautiful gardens. The view from the front of the castle is quite magnificent.

When you have visited the castle, retrace your steps to the Hunter's Path and resume the walk. At the end of the promontory, the path turns sharp right just below the castle. At the end, go through a gate onto a road and turn sharp left (signposted to the Fisherman's Path). Follow the road down the valley and cross a cattle grid. A short distance beyond the cattle grid turn left off the road onto a track, following the footpath sign.

At the end of the track, at a house called Gibhouse, fork left onto a path, again following a footpath sign. Cross a V-stile and when you reach the river turn left (signposted to Fingle Bridge). Do not cross the iron footbridge, but keep to the left-hand bank. This is the start of a lovely stretch through the woods, with the river gliding and tumbling down on your right.

After about 700m you go through a gate. A little way beyond you come to some steep steps leading high up the hillside, but you can avoid them by following the lower path across some rather rough rocks alongside the river. After a while you come to some more steps; you should take these as the path alongside the river has become eroded.

Some 2.5km (1^1/$_2$ miles) after joining the Fisherman's Path, you come to a kissing gate leading onto a road. Go through it and turn left. After about 100m you will see a footpath leading sharp left off the road (signposted to the Hunter's Path, the road near Castle Drogo and Drewsteignton). Take this for a lovely walk back to Drewsteignton through the woods, avoiding the road (which can become rather busy and therefore unpleasant to walk along, especially at

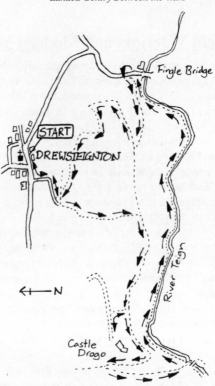

weekends). If you would prefer to avoid the steep climb up to the Hunter's Path, however, you can continue along the road for another 500-600m and then turn left into the woods.

The climb up the hill is stiff initially, but after a while it levels out somewhat and becomes less steep. The best thing is to take it slowly and pause from time to time to enjoy the birdsong. Just as you begin to think you will never reach the top, you leave the wood and an excellent view opens up ahead of you.

At the path junction, turn right (signposted to Drewsteignton). The path takes you back into the wood for a nice cool, gentle amble after your exertions. The path curves round the hill, and if you look to your right across the valley, you will see the ramparts of Prestonbury Castle, an Iron Age hill fort, on the top of the hill opposite. (For more information on Iron Age hill forts, see Walk 20.)

As you come round the hill, you cross a track. Go straight across, following the path sign, into a conifer wood. You cross a rivulet and continue round the hill on the other side. After a while you join a track. Go right and descend steeply to the valley below. At the bottom, go straight on (signposted to Drewsteignton). At the path junction at the end, go right (signposted to Drewsteignton again).

You are now back on your outward route, so follow the track up the hill to the road. Turn right and then left to return to the village square.

—— 20. Ancient Warriors and Modern Monks ——

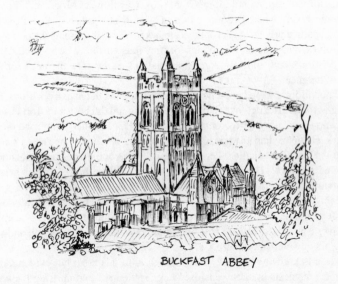

BUCKFAST ABBEY

———————————— THE BACKGROUND ————————————

Combining as it does visits to an ancient hill fort and a modern abbey, this final walk brings together different themes in the history of the Dartmoor area, the ancient and the modern, the religious and the secular.

Ancient Warriors. There were two Iron Age immigrations into Britain. The first group, known as Iron Age A, were mainly farmers who settled peacefully among the Bronze Age inhabitants and appear to have integrated with them. There is certainly no evidence of any conflict. (For more information on this group, see Walk 3.)

The second wave (Iron Age B) arrived from north-west France in the third century BC, and they were very different from the earlier settlers. They were essentially warriors; their aim was conquest not integration. Their arrival therefore introduced a new factor into the hitherto comparatively peaceful local scene - the dangers of war and the consequent need for defensive fortifications. For although there is evidence of the manufacture of weapons in other parts of Britain during the Bronze Age, none has been found in the Dartmoor area. The invaders introduced the horse and chariot into Britain, which gave them considerable mobility in warfare. Their main offensive weapon was a long iron sword, and in the defence of the hill forts they used slings armed with pebbles, with a range of about 100m.

Presumably because of the inhospitable climate and terrain, they did not settle on Dartmoor itself - there appear to have been few settlements of any kind

89

there at that time. But there are the remains of about twenty hill forts on the fringes of the moor, including Cranbrook Castle near Moretonhampstead, Prestonbury Castle near Drewsteignton and Hembury Castle near Buckfast. Most of these, particularly the most sophisticated, were certainly built by the newcomers themselves, but some of the simpler fortifications may have been erected by the mixed Bronze Age and Iron Age A populations as they felt the need for some kind of defence.

The hill forts were large enclosures built in good defensive positions, often on high ground. The defences consisted of banks and ditches; some forts had just one rampart, others had two, and they were usually of earth or stone, or a mixture of both. Hembury has just one, enclosing an area of about 3 hectares (7 acres). There is also what is called a counter-scarp - a second, lower bank outside the surrounding ditch. The rampart would probably have had a timber or stone breastwork at the top. The entrance is on southern side, approached via a wide causeway across the ditch, and would have been protected by a solid wooden gate. It would have been difficult to attack, as the ground falls away steeply to the River Dart on the eastern side and to the Holy Brook to the south and west, ruling out any element of surprise.

Little is known about life in the hill forts in this area, but evidence from elsewhere suggests that they enclosed large settlements, comprising the homes of the local chief and his dependants. They were therefore not just refuges in times of war but permanent centres from which the inhabitants went out each day to graze their stock and cultivate their crops.

Modern Monks. In the past, religious houses had a significant impact on the life of Dartmoor, both as landowners and as sources of spiritual guidance. There were four which had a particular influence - Tavistock and Buckland abbeys in the west, Plympton Priory in the south and Buckfast Abbey in the east - of which only Buckfast remains as a working monastery.

The original abbey at Buckfast is believed to have been founded in 1018, during the rule of King Knut (Canute). It was endowed with extensive lands, some as far away as the northern edge of the moor. But it was abolished in 1539, at the time of the dissolution of the monasteries under Henry VIII, and its various land holdings appropriated. The abbey buildings were gradually demolished by the new owners, until nothing remained of the original establishment.

The site was acquired by the Roman Catholic Church again towards the end of the last century, and in 1882 the first monks arrived to re-establish the community. They discovered the foundations of the medieval abbey church under their vegetable garden, and it was decided to rebuild it on the same site. It took five of the monks, only one of whom was trained as a stonemason, thirty-two years to complete, from 1906 to 1938. It was a somewhat precarious undertaking financially, as it was funded entirely from donations - Abbot Vonier, who initiated the project, is said to have started with a sovereign and a horse and cart. He lived just long enough to see his vision become reality, dying within weeks of the church's completion.

The result of this labour of love is a magnificent building containing some fine artworks, many created by the monks themselves, including beautiful mosaics and stained-glass windows. The abbey is also famed for its tonic wine and it bees - indeed, Brother Adam, who died recently, was a world authority on bees and bee-keeping.

THE WALK

Start and finish: Hembury Woods. Grid reference 728680
Parking: There is a car park and picnic area in the woods.
Length: 8.75km (5½ miles)
Approximate time: The walk itself will take about 2 -3 hours, but you should allow yourself adequate time to explore the Buckfast Abbey complex. This could vary from 20 minutes for a quick visit to the abbey church to an hour or more if you want to take in the shops and the exhibition.
Degree of difficulty: B
Route summary: This very attractive walk takes you through the delightful Hembury Woods, a National Trust property which has been designated a Site of Special Scientific Interest, down quiet country lanes bordered by flower-filled hedgerows and along a lovely stretch of riverbank. There is, however, a price to be paid: there are several stiff climbs.

Cross the road from the car park to follow a broad path through the wood on the other side. After about 100m, you will see a post on your right, with an arrow pointing left to the fort. Turn left for the first of the climbs. (If you want to extend your walk, you can continue along the path to the river and then cut up to the fort; the paths are clearly waymarked.)

The path is not too steep initially, and there is plenty of interest as you climb, in the form of wild flowers below you and birdlife above. You cross a track, after which the slope becomes steeper. At the top you come to another track. Turn right, following the arrow pointing to the fort again. Cross a stile and up ahead you will see the ramparts of Hembury Castle. Follow the path along the causeway over the ditch and through the wall.

A track runs across the middle of the area, but you are free to wander through the enclosure at will; in fact it is quite interesting to follow the wall and ditch round to get a better idea of the extent of the place. Towards the left of the enclosure you will see a mound. This was the site of a small medieval motte and bailey castle; it probably had a wooden keep in the middle, with a wooden palisade on the earth bank you can see surrounding the central mound.

To leave the fort, go through a kissing gate at the opposite end from where you entered it and follow the track on the other side. Go through a low bank and follow the track to a gate leading to a road. Turn right. As you follow the road, you will get some very good views over the moors on your left and farmland on your right. After about 600m, turn left down a pretty side lane and follow it down as it swings to the right to cross a stream and then to the left to follow the valley on the other side.

You pass a farm on your left and then start to climb steadily up a hill. It is a long ascent, but at the top you are rewarded by a superb view ahead and to your left. At the T-junction turn left (signposted to Buckfastleigh). There is another good view ahead of you, over farms and woods.

After about 400m, turn left down a narrow lane (signposted to Higher Mill Leat). Although you are descending steadily all the time, the views over the hedges are still excellent. After a while the lane becomes steeper, and at the bottom of the hill it turns sharp right to a stream. Just before it turns right again, turn off left through a gate (signposted to Burchetts Lodge for Buckfast). This leads you across a footbridge into a lovely stretch of woodland, where you follow a track alongside the Holy Brook.

After a while the brook curves away to the left, although you can still see it across the field below you. The track begins to climb up to the right, and meets another track at the top. Turn left here and go down through a gate to a road. Turn left again.

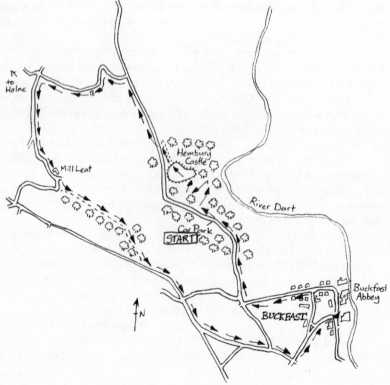

At the crossroads about 600m down the road, go straight on (signposted to Buckfast and Buckfastleigh). Keep following the road for just over 1km (¹/₂mile) more, ignoring the turnings to the right and the left, until you come to another crossroads. Turn left here (signposted to Buckfast). As you go down the hill, Buckfast Abbey comes into view ahead of you, and you also get some very good views beyond it.

Follow the road down and you will find the entrance to the abbey complex on your left. Go through the car park and under an archway by the gift shop to visit the magnificent church. There are also shops of various kinds you can visit, an exhibition and a very good restaurant, so there is a lot to explore if you are so minded.

To leave the complex, do not go back the way you came in, but turn right by the little Methodist chapel and go through another archway into Buckfast Road. Follow the road round to the left, and at the junction go straight on up Grange Road. After some distance, this takes you out of the village.

At the junction just outside the village, follow the main road round to the right, and at the next junction turn right (signposted to Hembury Woods). This pretty lane takes you between banks and hedges down to cross a stream and up into the woods on the other side. The climb up into the woods is steep, but mercifully it is relatively short. As it levels off, you will see the car park and picnic area on your left.

BIBLIOGRAPHY

The following is a selection of books that I have found particularly useful and interesting, both as general reading and with specific reference to the subjects discussed in the introductions to the various walks, and I recommend them to anyone interested in delving deeper into Dartmoor's past. Some of the older publications are now out of print and only available through libraries, but the more popular and important ones are reissued from time to time by local publishers.

Bennie, Michael, *Walking the Stories and Legends of Dartmoor* (Peninsula Press, 1995)

Butler, Jeremy, *Dartmoor Atlas of Antiquities* 5 volumes (Devon Books, 1991-7)

Crossing, William, *Crossing's Guide to Dartmoor.* (1912 edition. Reprinted by Peninsula Press, 1990)

Ewans, M.C., *The Haytor Granite Tramway and Stover Canal* (David & Charles,1964)

Fleming, Andrew, *The Dartmoor Reaves* (Batsford, 1988)

Fox, Aileen, *Prehistoric Hillforts in Devon* (Devon Books, 1996)

Gill, Crispin (ed.), *Dartmoor, a New Study* (David & Charles, 1970)

Greeves, Tom, *The Archaeology of Dartmoor from the Air* (Devon Books, 1985)
  Tin Mines and Miners of Dartmoor 2nd ed. (Devon Books, 1993)

Hambling, Paul, *The Dartmoor Stannaries* (Orchard Publications, 1995)

Harris, Helen, *The Haytor Granite Tramway and Stover Canal* (Peninsula Press, 1994)
  The Industrial Archaeology of Dartmoor, 4th ed. (Peninsula Press, 1992)

Hawkings, David J., *Water from the Moor* (Devon Books, 1987)

Hemery, Eric, *High Dartmoor: Land and People* (Hale, 1983)
  Walking Dartmoor's Ancient Tracks (Hale, 1986. Paperback edition 1997)
  Walking the Dartmoor Railroads, revised ed. (Peninsula Press, 1991)
  Walking the Dartmoor Waterways, revised ed. (Peninsula Press, 1991)

Higham, R.A., *Okehampton Castle* (English Heritage, 1984)

Hoskins, W.G., *Devon* (First published 1954. Reprinted by Devon Books, 1992)

Kendall, H.G., *The Plymouth and Dartmoor Railway* (Oakwood Press, 1968)

National Trust, *Castle Drogo* (The National Trust, 1995)

Pettit, Paul, *Prehistoric Dartmoor* (First published 1974. Reprinted by Forest Publishing, 1995)

Shepherd, Eric E., *The Plymouth & Dartmoor Railway and the Lee Moor Tramway* (ARK, 1997)

Stanbrook, Elisabeth, *Dartmoor Forest Farms* (Devon Books, 1994)

Stanes, Robin, *A History of Devon* (Phillimore, 1986)

Starkey, H.F., *Exploring Dartmoor* (Published privately, 1980)
  Exploring Dartmoor Again (Published privately, 1981)

Thurlow, George, *Thurlow's Dartmoor Companion* (Peninsula Press, 1993)

Wade, E.A. *The Redlake Tramway and China Clay Works* (Twelveheads Press, 1982)

Worth, R. Hansford, *Worth's Dartmoor* (First published 1953. Reprinted by Peninsula Press, 1994)

INDEX